ART DECO
ARCHITECTURE
ACROSS CANADA

ART DECO ARCHITECTURE ACROSS CANADA

Stories of the country's buildings
between the two World Wars

Tim Morawetz
Foreword by Alastair Duncan

Published by Glue Inc.
1920 Yonge Street, Suite 213
Toronto, Ontario M4S 3E2 Canada
www.glue-to.com/artdecoarchbook

Frontispiece photograph: Front entrance to Marine Building,
355 Burrard Street, Vancouver, B.C. McCarter & Nairne, 1929–30.
Photograph by Colin Rose and Sandra Cohen-Rose.

Design by Frank Mazzuca and Sabrina Berlato
Mazzuca Design, Photography & Ideas Inc.
Kleinburg, Ontario – www.mazzuca-dpi.com

Printed in Canada by Friesens
Typeset in ITC Kabel, Trade Gothic, and Bodega Sans
Printed on 80 lb., FSC-certified Garda Silk stock

Library and Archives Canada Cataloguing in Publication

Morawetz, Tim, 1958-, author
    Art deco architecture across Canada : stories of the country's
buildings between the two world wars / Tim Morawetz.

ISBN 978-0-9812413-1-9 (hardcover)

1. Art deco (Architecture)--Canada. 2. Architecture--Canada
--History--20th century. I. Title.

NA745.5.A7M67 2017   720.971'09042   C2017-903986-5

First Edition

For my wife Sue and my sons Stewart and James

Contents

Foreword

By Alastair Duncan

In the following pages, Tim Morawetz expands on his important first book, *Art Deco Architecture in Toronto* (2009), to provide an encyclopedic review of the Art Deco style of architecture in its multitude of interpretations across the entire Canadian nation. Included is the entire gamut of building types – office towers, banks, factories, town halls, museums, libraries, churches, homes and apartment buildings, department stores, transportation terminals, cinemas and hockey rinks – that were conceived and constructed during the interwar years and into the early 1950s, at which point architecture in Canada, as in other countries, was supplanted by the International Style, whose mandate was the elimination of all ornamentation, new or old.

The first challenge for 1920s architects in Canada, as elsewhere, was to cease being copyists of the past – to recognize that the periods in which these ancient forms had adequately served had long since passed. Their task was to develop an appropriate new means of artistic expression that was suited to contemporary society. Neoclassical columns and entablatures, Gothic flying buttresses and gargoyles, and all the standard Beaux-Arts motifs that adorned existing edifices were deemed *passé* – stylistic remnants of bygone eras. But forgoing historical influences with which to decorate modern buildings was one thing; finding satisfactory substitutes was quite another. It was for this reason that most of the nation's architects began, ironically, by looking back at Europe because, as one critic noted: "they do these things better there." The result was that much of Canada's architectural style from the mid-1920s was influenced by the high-style decorative vernacular emanating from the annual Paris Salons and the city's 1925

Exposition internationale des arts décoratifs et industriels modernes. Canada's architects and their draftsmen were drawn to a vast repertoire of Jazz Age motifs – including chevrons, scrolls, tiered fountains, sunbursts, cloud patterns, compacted floral bouquets, and the ubiquitous *biche* (doe) – that were plucked directly from illustrations in contemporary architectural magazines and trade journal advertisements. Within a few years, these decorative elements were being applied to all manner and size of buildings in Canada, as they were elsewhere, most notably in the United States and in current or former colonies of France and Britain.

Two names stand out amongst those who designed the architectural ornamentations found in these pages: John McIntosh Lyle and Charles Comfort. In the late 1920s and 1930s, these men created a range of bas-relief panels, decorative friezes and metal grilles that – in their interpretation of the high-style Art Deco grammar of decorative ornament they had appropriated from Paris – rivalled the murals and statuary by Lee Lawrie, Leo Friedlander, and Hildreth Meiere adorning Manhattan's Rockefeller Center, the pride of the parallel American Art Deco movement. Both men added an extra dimension to the subject matter of many of their compositions: images of regional and national significance. Lyle was especially drawn to depictions of Canadian flora and fauna; his Bank of Nova Scotia Building in Halifax reportedly contained 86 different examples of Canadian mammals, marine creatures, and plants. Comfort was more inclined to depict Canadian industry – as seen in the giant frieze, murals, and metal roundels of the Toronto Stock Exchange – as well as to capture the flavour of daily life across the country in the murals

Zigzag – as an overall building style – was in vogue from the mid-1920s until shortly after the start of the Depression; Streamlined Moderne arrived at the start of the Depression and lasted until the arrival of the International Style; and Stripped Classical can be found throughout the Art Deco era, since its use was more a function of the nature of the building or its owner, than chronology per se.

It's important to note that buildings from the Art Deco period frequently incorporated attributes from more than one of these styles. This should not surprise us, since these stylistic categories were established decades after the buildings were designed. At the time, commentators tended to describe these works as modern, moderne, or modernistic.

The remainder of this section presents the author's perspective on the key characteristics of each of these three styles

ZIGZAG: CONFIDENTLY REACHING FOR THE SKY

Ask the average person to name an Art Deco building and chances are they'll come up with a New York City skyscraper such as the Empire State Building or the Chrysler Building. The towering stature of such Zigzag-style buildings is a testament to the economic optimism of the era, while their jazzy, populist decoration speaks to the spirit and energy of the Roaring Twenties. Although the economic plunge after the October 1929 stock market crash essentially spelled the end of Zigzag skyscrapers, the motifs of Zigzag continued to be used on some buildings for years afterwards. There are six fundamental characteristics of the Zigzag style:

SYMMETRY: The façades of Zigzag buildings, and usually their floor plans, were generally symmetrical. This evolved from the Beaux-Arts era, when designers followed time-honoured, classical planning principles.

VERTICALITY: The predominant direction on Zigzag façades was vertical, with windows arranged in vertical strips (not horizontal bands), often separated by stone or brick piers. Other vertical elements included columns or pilasters flanking an entrance, or even modest protruding or incised lines in brickwork or stone. This vertical emphasis sought to increase the perceived height of the building, thus reinforcing the building's implied message of power or wealth.

ZIGZAG: Symmetry and verticality

Defining Art Deco Architecture

STEP-BACK MASSING: The massing of taller buildings from the 1920s, as well as that of some lower-rise structures, resembled a wedding cake or stepped pyramid, in which the building's façade was increasingly set back as it rose in height. This pattern of setbacks originally arose from zoning laws enacted in New York City in 1916, which sought to prevent streets from becoming dark and canyon-like. However, step-backs soon caught on as a purely visual device. On a small scale, step-back massing can be seen on cornice or lintel details.

MULTIPLE PLANES: Rarely was a wall on a Zigzag building a single flat surface. Façades usually incorporated two or more closely spaced planes – especially around doors and windows, and at the building's corners – to add visual interest and create dramatic shadow lines. Multiple planes can be thought of as step-back massing on the surface of the wall.

MATERIALS: Zigzag buildings constructed for wealthier clients often incorporated expensive interior finishes as exotic woods, distinctive stone trim, and luxurious wall fabrics; many buildings from this period incorporated newly invented, mass-produced materials such as artificial stone, vitrolite, glass block, monel metal, and stainless steel.

ZIGZAG: Step-back massing

ZIGZAG: Multiple planes

ZIGZAG: Materials

DECORATION: This is the richest attribute of Zigzag-style buildings, and so warrants more thorough explanation. There are three aspects of Zigzag decoration:

LOCATION: Decoration on the exterior of Zigzag buildings was generally found around the main entry, at the roofline, on the corners, and around or between vertical strips of windows (on the spandrel panels). Beyond the floor, walls and ceiling, interior elements such as light fixtures, elevator doors, door handles, and air grilles were frequently decorated.

TREATMENT: For the most part, Zigzag-style decoration was the opposite of its direct predecessor, Art Nouveau, characterized by natural materials and sinuous curves. Zigzag decoration was vigorous and flattened, often with polished or machined surfaces. When the decoration involved colour, hues were generally bold and bright.

SUBJECT MATTER: A study of the enormous variety of decorative motifs found on Canadian Zigzag buildings can be made simpler by organizing them into groups. Once again, this form of classification has its limitations, since the decoration on buildings usually drew upon more than one category. Nevertheless, the following framework may be helpful:

UNIVERSAL ZIGZAG MOTIFS: There are certain decorative elements that are present on Zigzag buildings around the world. These include representations of frozen fountains, sunbursts, lotus leaves, palmettes and stylized flowers, exotic animals such as the *biche* (doe), and the human figure (especially female nudes).

*S.S. Kresge Store, Victoria (reinstalled), 1930.
Architect: Garnet Andrew McElroy
Photo: Marilyn Welch

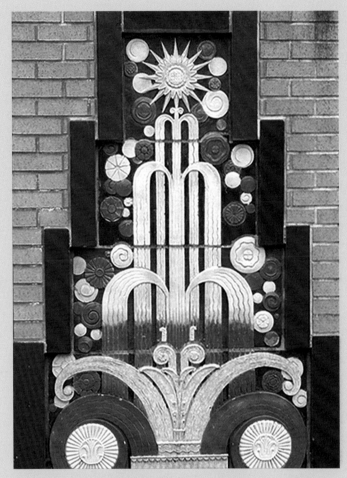

ZIGZAG DECORATION: Universal motif (frozen fountain)*

ZIGZAG DECORATION: Universal motif (lotus leaves)

Defining Art Deco Architecture

PURE GEOMETRY: Some Zigzag decoration consisted of merely geometric figures. This included incised or painted linear patterns, as well as flat, three-dimensional, or multiple layers of circles, semicircles, squares, rectangles, triangles, diamonds, hexagons, chevrons, or zigzags.

CLASSICAL MOTIFS: Symbols from antiquity – most commonly mythological gods and goddesses – adorned some Zigzag buildings. Usually heroic in scale and treatment, they sought to convey a sense of strength or authority. Other archetypal symbols that can be found include the cornucopia (horn of plenty) used as a symbol of abundance, and the owl as a symbol of wisdom.

HISTORY AND GEOGRAPHY: The decorative friezes, murals, or carvings on some Zigzag buildings told stories connected to the structure's geographic location, the history of its owner, as well as representations of First Nations peoples associated with its location.

FLORA AND FAUNA: Zigzag buildings occasionally incorporated depictions of the natural world – plants and animals – connected with the building's location.

ZIGZAG DECORATION: Pure geometry

ZIGZAG DECORATION: Classical motifs (Neptune and Rhea)*

ZIGZAG DECORATION: History and geography (Captain George Vancouver)

ZIGZAG DECORATION: Fauna (Atlantic fish)

ZIGZAG DECORATION: Flora (Canada lilies, sunflowers, and corn)**

*Bank of Nova Scotia, Toronto, 1946–51 Sculptor: Frederick Winkler
**Dominion Bank, Toronto, 1929. Design: John M. Lyle

LIFE AT
WORK

This chapter features Art Deco buildings where Canadians earned their living – in downtown offices high above the street; in banks and other institutions where financial affairs were managed; in factories where raw materials, consumer goods, or the day's news was processed and disseminated; or in government offices where services for the public were organized and delivered.

Concourse Building

100 Adelaide Street West, Toronto, Ontario

Baldwin & Greene, 1928; rebuilt 2015–17

Although Montreal was the leading city for commerce in Canada until well after World War II, Toronto was still an important centre for business and industry during the interwar years. Its natural harbour and a network of long-distance railway lines facilitated the arrival of raw materials and immigrants, the export of timber and other goods, and the building of warehouses. The Great Fire of 1904 – together with the economic boom of the later 1920s – prompted the construction of many high-rise offices surrounding the intersection of King and Bay Streets.

The first Art Deco office building in Toronto's downtown core was the Concourse Building, designed in 1928 by Martin Baldwin of Baldwin & Greene. (Baldwin went on to become the director of the Art Galley of Toronto, today's Art Gallery of Ontario.) Located at the northwest corner of Sheppard and Adelaide Streets, two blocks from the heart of the business district at King and Bay, the Concourse was developed by the Adelaide Sheppard Co. Ltd. as a speculative office tower. Unlike other skyscrapers of its time, it avoided the use of step-backs over its 16-storey height, since these would have diminished the amount of rentable space. The building's narrower southern façade – facing Adelaide, the more prestigious address – contained a two-storey arched front entrance that was flanked by retail spaces.

The Concourse's three-storey cast-stone base had Romanesque echoes, while the shaft was more Zigzag in style, boasting uninterrupted vertical lines of beige brick framing metal-sashed windows, separated by pale green spandrel panels. Topping the southern and eastern façades were giant coloured tiles in geometric designs inspired by First Nations art. Between these tiles were concrete panels containing raised wheat sheaf sculptures.

RIGHT The uninterrupted flow of the original Concourse Building's 16-storey façade is evident in this view from the 1980s. Notice that on the sunlit south façade, the beige-brick piers are unevenly spaced, with four windows of equal width in the centre bay, but only three windows at either side.

Concourse Building

The brightly coloured, glass-tile mosaics at the front entrance were the highlight of the building. Created by Group of Seven artist J.E.H. MacDonald and his son Thoreau, the seven panels forming the underside of the arch presented scenes of industry and transportation, while the larger panel above the entrance depicted the coming together – the concourse – of earth, fire, air, and water. Canadian poetry was chiselled into the walls of the entrance foyer.

Designated under Part IV of the Ontario Heritage Act in 1975, the aging but still beautiful structure was purchased in 1998 by Oxford Properties, which sought to demolish the tower as part of the redevelopment scheme for an entire city block. Arguing that the Concourse's ceiling heights were too low to function as modern office space, and that the location of its washrooms on the stair landings between floors was unworkable, Oxford's scheme promised to 'recreate' the Concourse and restore as much of its decoration as possible.

Despite the valiant efforts of a group of concerned citizens named 'Friends of the Concourse' who proposed alternatives to the building's destruction, Toronto City Council voted 38-12 on May 10, 2000, to permit its demolition.

While the Concourse remained standing for more than a decade on borrowed time, several designs for the new development were completed and refined. Economic conditions had finally improved such that, in July 2013, careful dismantling began of key elements that would be reinstalled in the new building. The new EY Tower, designed by Kohn Pederson Fox with WZMH Architects, is an angular, 40-storey, glass-skinned building that is set to open in 2017.

LEFT This 1980s photo shows the dazzling mosaics at the front entrance, created by artist J.E.H. MacDonald and his son Thoreau. The seven coffer panels depict (from left) an airplane, a ship, a winged automobile tire, a wheat sheaf and plough, a doe (or biche, a popular symbol in French Art Deco) a steam shovel, and atmospheric forces. The larger panel below represents the concourse of earth, fire, air, and water. In the rebuilt Concourse, the doors and frames have been re-created to match their original appearance.

The re-created Concourse Building occupies the southeast corner of the footprint of the new tower. While its original height has been maintained, it now contains only 14 floors, meaning its new window and spandrel heights have been stretched. Nevertheless, considerable steps were taken to recapture the original building's glory, including cleaning and returning the original mosaics to the front entrance, and uncovering and restoring several plaster ceiling murals from the former entrance lobby.

ABOVE Between the boldly coloured, First Nations – inspired tiles topping the brick piers are decorative concrete panels with wheat sheaf motifs that were originally gilded. Here at the southwest corner, the '2-3-2' lateral pattern of the windows corresponded with the number of vertical grooves in the green, solid-concrete spandrel panels. The narrow brick piers separating the windows are set at a 45-degree angle for added visual impact.

ABOVE Expecting that another skyscraper would soon be built to the west, the only decoration on the Concourse's western façade was found at the roofline and consisted of a pair of glazed-brick thunderbirds that flank a central sun motif with circling ravens. The thunderbirds and sunburst have been restored and reinstalled at the building's ground level, now visible to drivers entering the underground parking garage.

ABOVE On the rebuilt Concourse, the coloured tile motifs at the major piers have been restored and reinstalled, while those in-between needed to be re-created. The wheat sheath reliefs were formed from rubber moulds taken of the originals, and were re-gilded with 24-oz karat gold. The projecting spotlights that illuminate the decorated roofline, seen here in October 2016, are not original.

Price Building

65 St. Anne Street, Quebec City, Quebec

Ross & Macdonald, 1929–31

Propelled by its booming lumber trade, Quebec City had grown to become the third-largest port in North America by the early nineteenth century. The industry leader was William Price, a shrewd British-born businessman who milled wooden planks and exported squared timber to overseas clients, including the Royal Navy's shipyards. At one point, Price – nicknamed 'the father of the Saguenay' – controlled some 20,000 square kilometres of forest, and dominated the lumber industry in the Saguenay region on the north shore of the St. Lawrence. In 1855, he bought out his partners and formed William Price and Sons.

By the 1920s, a fourth generation was involved in the business. The focus of the business had shifted from lumber to pulp and paper, and a new head office for the company was required. Against the wishes of their elderly father, Sir William Henry Price, who had wanted the new headquarters to return to their original location in Kénogami (now Jonquière), brothers John Herbert Price and Arthur Clifford Price decided instead to locate it in Quebec City. And rather than building in the existing business district on St. Pierre Street in Lower Town, they chose a site within the historic walls of the Old City, close to city hall.

The brothers awarded the design of the building to the prominent Montreal architectural firm of Ross & Macdonald, who created a striking 18-storey tower. Although heavily criticized for having to destroy two historic houses and for dominating its four- and five-storey neighbours, the plans for the Price Building (Édifice Price) were approved by city officials who were eager to project a progressive spirit for the city.

The cornerstone was laid on Black Tuesday (October 29, 1929), with the building being finally inaugurated in 1931. However, the Price family soon lost control of the company, which eventually became part of newsprint giant Abitibi-Price.

Today, the building is owned by the city of Quebec, and is managed by the real estate arm of the province's Caisse de dépôt et placement. A 260-square-metre apartment on the 16th and 17th floors – originally built for the Price family – was renovated in 2001 to become the official residence for the Premier of Quebec.

As part of Quebec City's 400th anniversary celebrations on July 12, 2009, tightrope walker Ramon Kelvink Jr. successfully traversed the 230-metre distance between the 13th floor of the Price Building and the 15th floor of the nearby Fairmont Château Frontenac hotel.

ABOVE This roundel of a First Nations man's face is one of several located between the second floor windows on the front façade. The matching roundel contains a woman's face.

TOP LEFT Like the legendary Fairmont Château Frontenac, the Price Building features a steeply pitched, château-style copper roof with a series of dormer windows. The two buildings dominate the skyline of Old Quebec.

BOTTOM LEFT The building's main entrance at 65 St. Anne Street is richly decorated with fan-shaped and spiral floral motifs.

RIGHT Elegant chandeliers and subtle stone pilasters enhance the vertical feeling in the long and narrow lobby. Six bas-relief metal panels on the foyer walls illustrate various aspects of the Price family's forestry enterprise; one shows horse-drawn sleighs hauling logs out of the wintry woods, while another silently captures sheets of water cascading over a hydro dam.

OPPOSITE The step-back massing, vertically arranged windows, and decorative program place the 18-storey Price Building firmly in the Zigzag skyscraper tradition. It is clad in grey limestone from Quebec and Ontario.

Marine Building

355 Burrard Street, Vancouver, B.C.
McCarter & Nairne, 1929–30

With the opening of the Panama Canal in 1914, Vancouver quickly became an important port for shipments to Europe. Thanks to the foresight of Captain J.W. Hobbs – together with financing arranged by Toronto bond house G.A. Stimson and Co. – the Marine Building was intended to be the city's most prestigious office building, bringing grain and lumber shipping, grain and lumber shipping companies, insurance brokers, and import / export merchants together under one roof.

Situated in the heart of the business district and adjacent to the waterfront, the 20-storey building was designed by the Vancouver firm of McCarter & Nairne. Construction began in 1929 and lasted 16 months; the cost to complete the structure was $2.3 million – $1.1 million over budget. The onset of the Depression meant that much of the tower lay vacant. The City of Vancouver declined an offer to purchase it for a million dollars to use as a city hall. Eventually, the Marine Building was sold in 1933 for just $900,000 to Vancouver entrepreneur Fred Taylor, with financial backing from Ireland's Guinness family (of beer fame).

According to its original promotional brochure, the Marine Building "is the largest, highest and most modern office building in Western Canada, and is only exceeded by one or two buildings in the Empire." The *Vancouver Sun's* opening-day supplement quoted the architect's description that the tower "suggests some great marine rock rising from the sea, clinging with sea flora and fauna, tinted in sea green, flashed with gold, at night a dim silhouette piercing the sea mists."

The most remarkable feature of the building – not to diminish its 'textbook' Zigag massing, vertical windows and two-storey foyer – is its remarkable marine- and technology-themed decoration, making it arguably Canada's best Art Deco skyscraper.

Created by 'Doc' Watson, C. Young, and J.D. Hunter at McCarter & Nairne, the building's rich palette of decoration is found at key locations on the exterior, including the front entrance, the lower floors of the base, and the cornice of each step-back. The flood of decoration continues inside the two-storey lobby, whose ornately bracketed ceiling is illuminated by sconce lights hidden behind protruding ship prows. The original lobby floor, featuring battleship linoleum from Scotland, has been replaced by a terrazzo floor with large astrological symbols, but the metal elevator doors bearing bas-relief marine

motifs are still intact. The tower even included a luxuriously furnished penthouse apartment, complete with a living room that offered stunning views of the harbour and surrounding downtown.

Several careful renovations and mechanical upgrades later, the Marine Building continues to be a sought-after office location, and is home to several restaurants on the ground floor. It has appeared in several films and television programs, including the long-running series *Smallville*, in which it was the headquarters for Clark Kent's *Daily Planet* newspaper.

ABOVE RIGHT State-of-the-art dirigibles, submarines, trains, and airplanes, rendered in terracotta, are located above the first floor of the building.

OPPOSITE The brown brick walls of the 20-storey Marine Building are accented by beige terracotta panels around the base and at the top of each section of the step-back façade.

TOP The brass trim surrounding the main entrance includes such ocean creatures as crayfish, snails, seashells, starfish, and turtles.

ABOVE Terracotta seahorses, geese, and leaping fish embellish the fourth-storey cornice of the angled base of the building.

Marine Building

ABOVE The double-height foyer, seen here from the mezzanine, boasts colourfully decorated upper walls and an ornate ceiling, illuminated by sconce lights concealed within the prows of ships.

RIGHT Above this ship-prow sconce light is an opening to the mezzanine passageway; its profile is repeated in other elements of the building, including the front doors. Notice the plentiful decoration on the sconce and ceiling brackets.

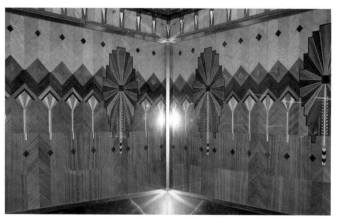

LEFT Marine-themed terracotta decoration literally surrounds the two-storey recessed entrance. The multicoloured screen above the revolving wooden doors features a sunburst with Captain Vancouver's ship at the centre, in front of which fly six stylized Canada Geese, which were once covered in gold leaf.

TOP Various types of underwater plants, crayfish, and other marine life populate the terracotta panels atop the front entrance.

ABOVE A dozen different local hardwoods were used in creating the inlaid geometric patterns inside the elevator cabs.

Aldred Building

507 Place d'Armes, Montreal, Quebec
Barott & Blackader, 1929–30

With business interests in Canada that included the Shawinigan Water and Power Company (a precursor to Hydro-Québec) and the Gillette Safety Razor Company, New York–based international finance firm Aldred & Company Ltd. required office space for its Canadian division. Eager to showcase the firm's wealth and influence, president John Edward Aldred envisaged a structure that would rival such Manhattan skyscrapers as the Barclay-Vesey Building, the Chrysler Building, and the Empire State Building.

Aldred hired Montreal-based architect Ernest Isbell Barott of Barott & Blackader to help realize his vision. Working with a site near the St. Lawrence River on the north side of Place d'Armes in Old Montreal, Barott sought to create a modern building that would "give consideration to the older buildings" in the historic square.

Thanks to the easing in 1927 of Montreal's bylaws that restricted building heights to 40 metres, Barott's earlier 12-storey design could now climb to a height of 23 storeys. Construction of the structural-steel tower began in July 1929 at the peak of the Roaring Twenties. The crash of the stock market three months later did not halt the $2.8-million project, which was finally completed in 1931. Aldred & Company occupied only a portion of the building, renting the remaining office space to legal and accounting firms.

To accommodate the site's oddly angled corner, the Aldred Building's walls are aligned with the street for three floors, then twist imperceptibly to be square to its neighbour, the Notre-Dame Basilica.

State-of-the-art amenities such as a central vacuum system, built-in ducts for electrical and telephone cables, an electric time-clock system, and six high-speed Otis Fensom elevators with teak interiors spoke to the modernity of Montreal's first Art Deco office tower.

RIGHT A symmetrical façade, step-back massing, and windows separated by protruding Indiana limestone piers make the 23-storey, steel-frame Aldred Building a classic Zigzag skyscraper.

ABOVE A carved screen depicting birds resting on hydro-electrical wires conceals a heating grille above the front vestibule doors. The exterior metalwork above the doors features the ubiquitous Deco spiral motif.

MIDDLE LEFT Typical Art Deco floral motifs decorate the top of the third level of the façade. Notice the mix of bas-relief geometric shapes and stylized flowers found on the spandrel panel.

LEFT The floor of the opulent main lobby boasts a repeating pattern of hexagons and triangles made from exotic marbles. Frosted glass sconce lights on octagonal marble backs illuminate the ceiling's stylized coffers. Notice the bold geometric pattern in the backlit stained-glass panel at the rear of the lobby.

Canadian General Electric Building

265 Notre Dame Avenue, Winnipeg, Manitoba
Northwood & Chivers, 1930

The completion of the Canadian Pacific Railway, together with the arrival of European immigrants in the last decades of the nineteenth century, prompted the diversification of Winnipeg's formerly distribution-based economy. The city's growth also spurred the adoption of new technologies, specifically electricity, that were already popular in Eastern Canada.

Due to surging commercial and residential demand for its electrical appliances and fixtures, Canadian General Electric decided in 1930 to expand its existing space and construct a new Winnipeg office on the fringes of the city's historic Warehouse District.

Not surprisingly, the building's design expressed the progressive Art Deco styling of the era. The ground floor contained showroom space, while the second floor housed offices furnished with battleship green linoleum – and, of course, excellent lighting! The company's mining machinery and other heavy electrical equipment was stored on the remaining three floors of the reinforced-concrete building, served by a 1,800-kilogram capacity freight elevator with a monorail system in the basement.

The building was renamed the Natural Gas Building in 1954 when taken over by the Winnipeg and Central Gas Company.

MIDDLE LEFT Traditional stylized floral, rosette, and scroll motifs adorn the pyramidal bronze screen above the main entrance.

BOTTOM LEFT Step-back massing and multiple-plane detailing accentuate the end bays of the façade. Notice the vertically fluted limestone spandrels that accentuate the building's height.

TOP The five-storey showroom, office and warehouse feature a smooth façade of Tee Pee Mocha brick rising above the one-storey Tyndall limestone base. On the protruding corner blocks, notice the sawtooth banding beneath the second-floor windows.

ABOVE RIGHT This original exterior light fixture features elegant geometric detailing. Notice the First Nations – inspired pattern in the stone molding above the lamp.

OPPOSITE Three sensational Art Deco bas-reliefs – portraying the three pillars of the 1930s Calgary economy – are located above the front façade's large upper-level windows. The upper panel displays oil gushing from the nearby well at Turner Valley. The middle panel portrays a sheaf of prairie wheat in front of a radiant sunset. The lower panel shows a rancher's saddle resting on a rail fence with the Rocky Mountains in the background.

ABOVE This original light fixture illuminated the steps down to the basement vault.

LEFT Splayed, carved-sandstone bas-reliefs frame the ground floor windows. The left one presents a view of traditional First Nations life on the prairies; it contains a bison head, an elder wearing a headdress, hunting tools, and a partially full vase of grain. The facing panel – depicting prairie life after European contact – features a horse head, rifles, a Stetson-wearing cowboy, scythes, and an overflowing vase of grain.

Bank of Montreal

144 Wellington St., Ottawa, Ontario

Barott & Blackader 1929–31

Seeking to capitalize on the expansion of local transportation networks and eastern Ontario's timber industry, Bank of Montreal – founded in 1817 – opened the first bank in Bytown (now Ottawa) in 1842.

A century later, the bank held a competition for a new building to replace its 1872 branch opposite Parliament Hill. Montreal architect Ernest Barott of Barott & Blackader won the competition with a monumental design that he described as "a modern interpretation of Greek design" – and what today can be termed Stripped Classical.

Above the front façade's tall windows are spectacular bas-relief sculptural panels depicting allegorical and Canadian historical themes that were crafted by American sculptor Emil Seiburn, who regularly worked for John D. Rockefeller.

The large central banking hall features a coffered plaster ceiling, marble floor with mosaic inlays, decorative metal chandeliers, and walls of Benedict stone that resembled Indiana limestone.

The building was recognized in 1932 with a Royal Architectural Institute of Canada gold medal, and received a Federal Heritage Building classification in 1986.

After having been vacant for several years, the building was rehabilitated and a western annex built. The Sir John A. Macdonald Building – unveiled in June 2015 – now serves as a federal government function and meeting space.

LEFT Located above the main entrance, this bas-relief panel, entitled 'Thrift,' was carved by American sculptor Emil Seiburn; it depicts a child being handed a precious jewel-like object.

TOP The Queenston limestone front façade of this Stripped Classical bank branch features tall vertical windows separated by incised pilasters with geometric capitals.

Bank of Nova Scotia Head Office and Halifax Main Branch

1709 Hollis Street, Halifax, Nova Scotia

John M. Lyle; Andrew R. Cobb (associate), 1930–31

New Year's Eve, 1831. A group of prominent Halifax merchants have gathered to discuss the need for a 'public bank' as an alternative to the privately owned Halifax Banking Company. Three months later, their goal was realized as the first branch of the Bank of Nova Scotia opened its doors in downtown Halifax.

By the late 1920s, when the bank had outgrown its previous head office and Halifax main branch at 188 Hollis Street, it hired architect John M. Lyle to design the new building. Its function requirements were simple: a spacious banking hall on the ground level, with four storeys of rental office space above. The resulting design was, in the words of Geoffrey Hunt – the guest curator of the first major exhibition of Lyle's work – "a grand synthesis of Lyle's architectural ideas and goals."

The Stripped Classical treatment of the steel-frame structure projected an image of stability and solidity that suited the stature of the bank and its location adjacent to Halifax's iconic Province House. As with Lyle's Bank of Nova Scotia branch in Calgary (page 19), his commitment to Canadian-themed decoration was now fully realized.

The building has remained the Halifax main branch ever since its opening day on August 3, 1931, and is currently home to the bank's Atlantic Regional Office. The bank's head office moved to Scotia Plaza in Toronto – a new complex that was built around Lyle's 'big job' project. that he didn't live to see completed in 1951.

TOP The dozen spandrel panels on the Hollis Street façade feature wonderful bas-reliefs carved by prominent architectural sculptor Ira Lake. The cast of Canadian animals includes a turkey, bears, beavers, geese, owls, a swan, fish and an eagle, as well as a basket of flowers and a bundle of wheat.

LEFT This pair of fish is just one of the 86 different Canadian-themed motifs that grace the building. The molding above the sculpture is based on First Nations motifs.

Bank of Nova Scotia Head Office and Halifax Main Branch

ABOVE More colourful than most bank interiors, the 10-metre-high banking hall features flattened marble pilasters, as well as octagonal ceiling coffers containing bas-relief depictions of various animals. Notice the freestanding brass banking counters, and the octagonal frosted-glass chandeliers.

ABOVE RIGHT This bronze grille on a ground-floor window includes seahorses, turtles, frogs, and water lilies, centred on a trident.

ABOVE MIDDLE Lyle's decorative program also included scenes of the local maritime history and economy. This depiction of the Sydney steel mills in Cape Breton celebrates technology; the smoke belching out of the stacks is treated as an Art Deco flowing fountain. A wise owl watches the scene from above.

ABOVE LEFT The Bedford limestone principal façade on Hollis Street is a fine example of Stripped Classical design. The first two floors containing the double-height banking hall resemble the stone treatment found on the adjacent Province House. The upper four storeys feature a slightly protruding, three-bay frontispiece boasting flat fluted pilasters. Carved medallions of old French, English, Canadian, and Nova Scotian coins embellish the cornice frieze.

Huron & Erie Mortgage Corporation Building

220 Dundas Street, London, Ontario

Watt & Blackwell, 1930–31

Although the Fork of the Thames River location (present-day London, Ontario) missed out on being selected as the capital of Upper Canada, on January 30, 1826, it was named the administrative centre for central Western Ontario.

The 1850s arrival of the railways ushered in a period of economic growth, while the outbreak of the American Civil War in 1861 brought added prosperity to the region, as local wheat was shipped south to supply the Union Army. This greater affluence led a group of the city's merchants, in 1864, to form their own trust company: the Huron and Erie Savings and Loan Society. Shortly afterward, it merged with the London Permanent Building Society to form the Huron and Eric Mortgage Corporation, which, in 1901, established a trust subsidiary – the Canada Trust Company. (In 2000, Canada Trust merged with Toronto Dominion Bank to become today's TD Canada Trust.)

Having outgrown its previous premises, Huron & Erie set out in 1930 to build London's first 'skyscraper' at the northeast corner of Clarence and Dundas Streets. The nine-storey building included a ground-level banking hall with mezzanine; executive offices on the third floor; a staff dining room, assembly hall, and lounge area on the top floor; plus five floors of rental offices in-between. The basement contained safety deposit boxes and the vault, protected by timed locks plus 45-cm-thick reinforced concrete walls with an added steel-plate lining. Notably, the Huron & Erie building was western Ontario's first financial institution equipped with a night depository chute.

Based on its pivotal role in the formation of Canada Trust, it's no surprise that this building now houses a TD Canada Trust branch.

RIGHT The main entrance on Dundas Street consists of a two-storey Stanstead granite frontispiece that is flanked by a recessed stone detail topped by superb Art Deco geometric motifs. Simple grooves adorn the spandel panels; the solid marble panel above the entry once displayed 'The Huron and Erie Mortgage Corporation' in metal lettering.

ABOVE RIGHT Even the brass fire hose cabinet contains Art Deco decoration.

TOP A series of bas-relief panels above the mezzanine level of the façade – carved by American sculptor Ulysses Ricci – depict the various industries of Canada.

ABOVE LEFT The overall styling of the nine-storey building is restrained Zigzag. It features a light court on the west-facing façade to help illuminate and ventilate the interior offices.

ABOVE MIDDLE The main lobby features bronze elevator doors with multiple-plane, step-back marble surrounds. The doors are covered in typical floral and wave-shaped Art Deco motifs.

Toronto Stock Exchange

234 Bay Street, Toronto, Ontario
George & Moorhouse; with Samuel H. Maw (associate), 1937

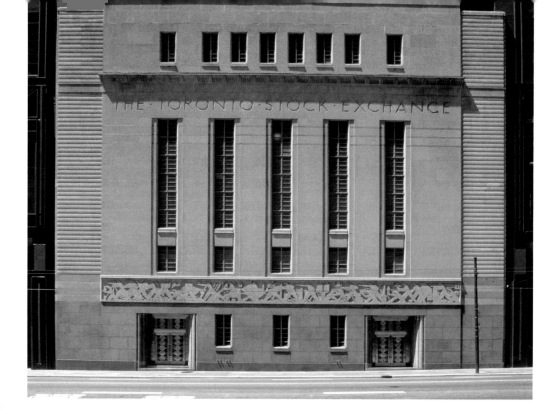

More than a year after the merger of the old Toronto Exchange and Standard Stock & Mining Exchange in 1934, the Managing Committee of the Toronto Stock Exchange decided to build a larger, more modern facility on the same site as its existing 1912 building, which had been designed by John M. Lyle. The firm of George & Moorhouse was selected to design the new building, together with associate Samuel H. Maw.

Their design needed to express the solidity and importance of the expanded Exchange in hard times while anticipating more prosperous days ahead, to match the scale of its (then) neighbours, and to reflect its location on Toronto's prestigious Bay Street. With a $750,000 pricetag, the building was a major project for its day, accounting for a significant proportion of Toronto's total construction activity in 1936–37.

To accommodate all the required functions on the tight lot, the trading floor with its 12-metre-high ceiling was located on the second floor, leaving the street level free for the members' dining room, luncheonette, coatrooms, and washrooms. Offices and meeting rooms were on the third floor, while the statistical, quotation and ticker services, staff lockers, and vaults were located in the basement. Three stairways, a passenger elevator, and a service elevator connected all the floors.

The most distinctive aspect of the Stock Exchange building is the decoration, created by Canadian painter, muralist, teacher, and commercial artist Charles Comfort who had been recruited by the building's chief designer, Samuel Maw. Most prominent is Comfort's 22.5-metre-long carved limestone frieze that graces the building's front façade. Representing a 'processional of industry,' it contains 31 life-size figures of labourers and white-collar workers. Specific figures from the frieze are isolated and presented in metal roundels on the two sets of entry doors, while eight of the industries that were represented on the Exchange are depicted in the painted canvas murals lining the east and west walls.

Quite apart from its visual merits, the Toronto Stock Exchange building was a marvel of contemporary communications and trading technology. Bid-and-ask prices were updated by operators in the basement and mechanically displayed on the faces of the nine hexagonal trading 'posts.' Traders at the nearly 200 telephone desks silently summoned their floor staff with special lights on giant 'annunciator' boards, while sales slips and messages were noiselessly transported using a network of pneumatic tubes.

Shortly after the Exchange's opening on March 30, 1937, a *Maclean's* magazine writer described it as "magnificent in architectural beauty; especially in its interior, in the perfection of conveniences for which it is designed, in the completeness of its equipment."

In 1978, the building was designated under the Ontario Heritage Act; it housed the TSE until 1983, when the institution moved to the Exchange Tower on King Street West. After lying vacant for several years, an agreement was signed with its purchasers, Olympia and York, to preserve and restore the building in return for obtaining the air rights above the building. Kuwabara Payne McKenna Blumberg Architects were hired in 1988 to renovate and enlarge the non-designated portions of the building in order to create the Design Exchange, which was formally opened by Prime Minister Jean Chrétien on September 21, 1994.

ABOVE The base of the three-storey façade is pink-coloured Brodies granite, with buff Indiana limestone above. The tall second-floor windows illuminate the Exchange's trading floor within. Interestingly, all three variants of Art Deco styling are found on the exterior. The existence of the carved frieze, together with the vertical proportion of the window openings, lends a Zigzag character; the pronounced cornice molding and classical lettering are Stripped Classical. But the building's dominant style is Streamlined Moderne, as seen in the flush stone speed-stripes at either end of the frieze and in the convex courses of stone at the sides that span the second and third floors.

TOP RIGHT Charles Comfort also painted the eight, five-metre-high canvas murals found between the windows on the east and west walls. In this view of the west wall, we see (from left) the murals depicting transportation and communications, pulp and paper, construction and engineering, and agriculture. The eastern murals depict oil, mining, smelting, and refining.

LEFT This archival view shows what the trading floor looked like when it first opened. Horizontal panels of flashed opal glass softened the light from the windows, then curved upward and continued across the ceiling to diffuse the artificial light from rows of fluorescent tubes. The effect was a continuous ribbon of light illuminating the space. The cork-tile flooring and acoustic-tile walls and ceiling dampened the noise made by hectic traders. Notice the steel speed-stripes on the walls, and the decorative horizontal bands gracing the since-removed phone desks.

ABOVE This Streamlined Moderne newel post, at the base of the staircase leading up to the trading floor, features a lacquered birch handrail and stainless steel bands. When first built, its central post was made of cast glass.

Toronto Stock Exchange

TOP LEFT Charles Comfort's sensational frieze, 22.5 metres in length, is located at the floor level of the trading floor. Its streamlined forms depict men working in the various industries that were traded on the Exchange. Carved with a pneumatic chisel, the frieze was completed by Peter Schoen in less than two months. Above the frieze, the bullnose framing around the horizontally proportioned, metal-sash windows enhance the streamlined effect.

RIGHT The smooth, low-relief surface of this stainless-steel door roundel, depicting mining, echoes the treatment of the limestone frieze above. Notice the angular pose of the worker, and the crisp styling of the drilling machine, mineshaft support pole and even the headlamp on the miner's helmet.

TOP RIGHT Each of the stainless-steel doors in the building's two entrances contains seven different roundels. Notice the granite engaged columns topped with metal speed-stripes flanking the doors.

TOP Step-back, multiple-plane limestone capitals adorn the slightly protruding brick pilasters separating the metal-sash industrial windows. The incised Christie's Biscuits sign on all four façades was still prominent as seen here in 1980 after the building had been sold.

BOTTOM The one-storey factory was clad in red brick from Redcliffe, Alberta, with local Tyndall limestone trim. The company's original blue, yellow, and white logo is visible in this early 1990s photo.

Campbell Soup Company of Canada

60 Birmingham Street, New Toronto, Ontario

Mathers & Haldenby, 1931

The company that evolved into the Campbell Soup Company began in 1869, when Joseph Campbell, a fruit merchant, and Abraham Anderson, an icebox manufacturer, teamed up and began making canned fruits and vegetable preserves at their factory in Camden, New Jersey.

In 1897, John T. Dorrance, a nephew of the general manager, joined the company. At age 24 with a chemistry degree from MIT, Dorrance invented condensed soup by finding a way to halve the amount of water in the company's soup cans – a breakthrough that led to lower shipping costs and a more affordable product for consumers. Soon, the company made 21 varieties of condensed soups – including, of course, tomato – which grocers sold for a dime per can.

The iconic red colour of the company's cans arrived in 1898, when a Campbell's executive was smitten by the carnelian red of Cornell University's football jerseys. Two years later, after winning the top prize at the 1900 Paris Exposition Universelle, a gold medallion was added to the label.

A major advertiser since its founding, the company gained free publicity in 1962, when American pop artist Andy Warhol produced his first silkscreen containing 32 different flavours of the Campbell's soup.

In November 1930, Campbell's launched its first foreign subsidiary in Canada, opening a factory and office nine months later in the town of New Toronto – a planned community focused on manufacturing, located southwest of downtown Toronto. Each fall, when the new crop of tomatoes arrived at the factory, the company would write 'help needed' messages in chalk on the sidewalks of Lake Shore Boulevard West.

The office on Birmingham Street continues to house the Campbell Company of Canada (with a much enlarged factory), although the eastern portion of the office façade was concealed behind a modern addition some years ago.

TOP The double-hung windows in the taller end wings are dramatically framed above and below by stone trim panels featuring giant convex fluting. The multiple planes of brick on either side add visual energy to the composition.

RIGHT Each bay of the two-storey, red-brick symmetrical façade (seen here in 1993, before the modern addition) contains three oversize windows, separated by slightly protruding brick piers capped with stone trim.

Canada Packers Plant

Fort Road NW, south of 70th Street NW, Edmonton, Alberta
Eric R. Arthur (with Anthony Adamson), 1936 (demolished 1995)

Canada Packers was formed in 1927 when overcapacity in the meatpacking industry prompted the merger of William Davies Company, Gunns Limited, and Harris Abattoir Company. The new firm immediately became Canada's largest food processing company – a title it would hold for six decades.

In the midst of the Depression, Canada Packers decided to build a $1-million packing plant in what was then North Edmonton, close to packing plants run by its competitors.

Toronto architecture professor Eric R. Arthur and partner Anthony Adamson consulted with equipment manufacturers, and studied facilities in the U.S., Great Britain, and Denmark to ensure their new plant would be on the cutting edge of factory planning; it earned a gold medal of merit from the Royal Architectural Institute of Canada in 1936. Although some commentators describe the factory as an early example of the International Style, its Streamlined Moderne features should not be overlooked.

Nearly 400 tradesmen worked to construct the building between March and November of 1936. The plant was capable of producing over 34,000 kilograms of smoked meats and nearly 23,000 kilograms of sausage and cooked meats per week, and featured separate shipping docks for coastal exports and local deliveries. The ground floor housed government inspection rooms, a separate dining room for women employees, plus a 'hospital with attendant' nurse. When it opened, the plant employed over 300 workers, which rose to more than 1,000 workers during its heyday from the 1950s through the early 1970s.

Industry changes led to the plant's closure and, ultimately, its demolition in 1995. Only the plant's 30-metre smoke stack remains standing in a barren field – a witness to this important structure.

TOP The three-storey factory featured a reinforced concrete structure supporting brick curtain walls laid in a German garden-wall pattern. This side view showcases the loading dock used for exports; the company's name was announced with two-metre-tall reinforced concrete letters.

RIGHT The circular shape of the canopy over the office entrance was matched by the curvature of the brick wall below. Most windows contained horizontally proportioned panes of glass; sections of brick with protruding speed stripes separated the front façade's second-floor windows and wraparound corner windows above.

The William H. Wright Building

140 King Street West, Toronto, Ontario
Mathers & Haldenby, 1937 (demolished 1974)

Born in London, Ontario, in 1905, George McCullagh got a taste of the newspaper business early on, having served as a local delivery boy for the *Globe*. At age 16, he became the company's subscription agent for London, and at 22 was named the paper's assistant financial editor covering the northern mining scene. After leaving the *Globe*, he worked on the floor of the Toronto Stock Exchange before partnering with Richard Barrett to form investment firm Barrett, McCullagh and Company. He was reportedly worth a million dollars by age 30.

In 1936, wishing to return to the newspaper business, McCullagh employed $1.85 million in financing provided by mining magnate William Henry Wright to purchase, in quick succession, the Liberal-allied *Globe* and the Conservative-allied *Mail and Empire*. He merged them into *The Globe and Mail* newspaper, and appointed himself publisher. McCullagh decided to construct a new building at the northeast corner of King and York Streets to house his new paper, and named it after his financial backer Wright.

In an August 1938 trade journal article, architect Alvan Mathers wrote that "...speed and punctuality is the keynote of the planning of a newspaper plant. The flow...must be rapid, continuous and uninterrupted." The prevailing architectural style of Streamlined Moderne was well suited to express this focus on efficiency. (By contrast, the *Toronto Star* building from 1929, located one block east, was a 23-storey tower whose massing and decorative treatment was more Zigzag in style.)

The newspaper operations employed all six floors of the building, which occupied the entire site. Mathers noted it was important to have plenty of daylight in most areas of the building, which explains the expanse of factory-like windows on its largely unadorned west façade. Artificial lighting and ventilation eliminated the need for interior light wells, while some interior spaces had glass-block partition walls.

Each night, crowds would gather on the York Street sidewalk and peer through the tall windows to watch the next morning's edition roll off the presses at a rate of 2,500 papers per minute.

For a Streamlined Moderne building, the structure contained an impressive amount of decoration. Flanking the main entrance were two large, Indiana limestone panels – designed by sculptor Frederick Winkler and carved in place by

Sebastiano Aiello – symbolizing the power of the press and its responsibility for protecting the public. Just above the entrance canopy were six life-size panels that depicted mining, fishing, agriculture, lumbering, aviation, and the fur trade.

Sadly, the structure lasted less than four decades before being demolished to make way for the First Canadian Place complex. However, the two entrance bas-reliefs were preserved, thanks to the foresight of Rosa Hewetson Clark and her husband, Spencer Clark. On numerous occasions, when landmark buildings in Toronto and elsewhere were being demolished, the Clarks claimed or purchased them, then installed them in a garden setting we now know as the Guild Park and Gardens in Scarborough, Ontario.

ABOVE This view of the double-height King Street main entrance showcases the low-relief sculptural panels that flanked the front doors. The newspaper's name was proudly announced in freestanding stainless-steel letters on the canopy above. The metal doors were saved and reinstalled on *The Globe and Mail*'s subsequent building on Front Street West.

Timmins Daily Press Building

1 Cedar Street, Timmins, Ontario

Sheppard & Masson, 1939–40 (demolished 1997)

This is the story of one of Canada's most important Art Deco buildings: how it came to be, and how it met its unfortunate end.

Roy Herbert (Roy) Thomson, the Toronto-born son of a barber, was unable to enlist in the Army during World War I due to bad eyesight, and instead attended a business college. After the war and an unsuccessful stint farming in Manitoba, he returned home, where, among other jobs, he sold radios for manufacturer De Forest Crosley Radios Limited in its only available territory, northern Ontario.

At the time, there were no radio stations in the region; local listeners could only receive a decent signal from U.S. stations, and from Toronto's CFRB in the evening. If Thomson was to succeed in selling more radios, more local signals were needed. Taking matters into his own hands, he paid nearby Abitibi Paper Company one dollar to rent its unused radio licence for a year, then purchased an old transmitter in Toronto for $200. On March 3, 1931, radio station CFCH took to the airwaves, broadcasting from North Bay, Ontario.

The following year, Thomson launched a second radio station, CKGB, in the town of Timmins. A gold-mining town, Timmins was founded in 1912; it was named after Noah and Henry Timmins, considered the founding fathers of Canada's mining industry. The presence of the 'The Big Three' – Dome Mine, Hollinger Gold Mine, and McIntyre Mines – as well as the forestry industry, meant that the Great Depression affected Timmins less than most other communities. Consequently, it experienced an influx of job seekers from the south; this created a more attractive market for Thomson's new radio station.

In 1933, Thomson launched a third station, CJKL in Kirkland Lake. Although he continued to sell radios for years afterwards, he increasingly focused on his own radio stations.

Always seeking new opportunities, in 1934 Thomson paid $200 plus several promissory notes to purchase the printing press from the defunct weekly newspaper, the *Timmins Citizen*. Within a year, he re-launched the paper as the *Timmins Daily Press*.

After a fire on April 2, 1939, destroyed the building in which the *Daily Press* and CKGB were housed, Thomson quickly set about rebuilding. He hired the Windsor,

Ontario–based architecture firm of Sheppard & Masson to design a thoroughly modern headquarters for his Northern Broadcasting & Publishing Company. For inspiration, the architects visited radio station designs in Detroit and New York City.

Construction was temporarily halted due to the outbreak of World War II, but resumed later that fall. On October 14, 1940, the *Daily Press* and CKGB – now affiliated with the CBC – celebrated the building's completion with an open house and public dance.

The ground floor housed the advertising and accounting offices, as well as the sizeable newspaper composing room. The daily listings for CKGB's national network evening programs were displayed on a theatre-style marquee over the station's entrance. On the second floor were three recording studios – the largest of which seated 150 people and contained a pipe organ and grand piano – plus the announcers' room, a central control room, and the spacious editorial room. The publisher had the prime corner office. A fully equipped, streamlined penthouse apartment on the third floor served as Thomson's home when he was in town.

ABOVE Housing the *Timmins Daily Press* newspaper and radio station CKGB, this remarkable Streamlined Moderne building featured a flat roof, raised period lettering above the curved corner front entrance, and stretches of vertically ridged wall decoration flanking the glass block windows. Its structure consisted of fireproof concrete plus structural steel; its exterior walls were composed of terracotta blocks finished with a rust-coloured 'crystalline' stucco. Thomson Corporation had vacated the building when these photos were taken in 1990.

Timmins Daily Press Building

The printing presses and mailing room were in the basement.

In the 1960s, legendary country musician Stompin' Tom Connors recorded his first '45' singles at the station. Meanwhile, esteemed journalist and broadcaster Peter Gzowski worked at the *Daily Press* in the mid-1950s.

Sadly, time was not kind to this iconic sstructure. As the Thomson Corporation's media empire expanded across Canada and internationally, the *Daily Press* did not receive the financial attention it deserved. In the 1980s era of word-processors, its reporters still crafted their stories on typewriters in deteriorating offices.

After being sold to a developer in 1984, the building lay vacant before being taken over by the city in 1994, with $85,000 owing in back taxes. Despite having been recognized in 1992 by the Historic Sites & Monuments Board of Canada as "one of Canada's finest examples of moderne architecture," the *Daily Press* building was demolished in 1997.

A section of the terrazzo floor from the entrance foyer, containing a compass-shaped motif, was preserved and displayed in the new *Timmins Daily Press* building constructed on Cedar Street South. But since Postmedia, the building's most recent owner, sold the paper in July 2016, the future of this last remnant of the once-magnificent structure remains uncertain.

ABOVE The terrazzo floor of the newspaper's front lobby featured a geometrical compass design.

RIGHT The kitchen in Roy Thomson's private apartment on the third floor featured streamlined counters, shelves, and indirect metal ceiling lights.

BOTTOM RIGHT Curved walls flank the recessed doorway into the second-floor foyer. Notice the glass-block sidelights and the round ceiling light fixture.

Toronto Postal Delivery Building

40 Bay Street, Toronto, Ontario

Charles Dolphin, 1939–40

A 1937 request from Canada's Postmaster General, together with a desire to stimulate Toronto's construction industry, led the federal Department of Public Works to commission the new Toronto Postal Delivery Building in 1938. It was not intended to serve as a public post office, but rather as a warehouse for the sorting and distribution of mail.

Architect Charles Dolphin completed the drawings and specifications in 1939; construction began that year before it was halted in 1940 when the federal government declared a moratorium to reduce non-war expenditures. Later that year, work resumed so the building could serve temporarily for 'war storage purposes.'

In 1946 it was returned to the Post Office Department, with space added at the roof level the following year, along with interior renovations to return it to its original use. Construction of the elevated Gardiner Expressway, which hems in the building to the south, began in the 1950s.

Situated just south of Union Station, the building was connected to the station by a tunnel running under the sizeable train shed, facilitating easy transfer of mail that travelled by train. Other mail arrived in postal vans, entering and exiting the building at the eastern and western ends of the south façade. Unsorted mail was first hoisted to the top floor by a conveyor belt, then descended through gravity-fed chutes while it was sorted by size and geography. Finally, the mail returned to the first floor for loading into postal vans for pickup and distribution.

Mail was sorted in the building for nearly 50 years, until Canada Post Corporation moved all its operations to a new facility in Mississauga, Ontario.

Designated by the City of Toronto under the Ontario Heritage Act in 1990, it was purchased by developers but then transferred back to Canada Post in 1993 before being sold to the Toronto Raptors basketball team the next year. The Raptors agreed to preserve the eastern and southern facades when building the new Air Canada Centre.

In 1998, Maple Leaf Gardens Ltd. (now known as Maple Leaf Sports & Entertainment Ltd.) purchased the building and the Raptors. In their first game in their new home on February 20, 1999, the Toronto Maple Leafs needed overtime to beat their perennial rivals, the Montreal Canadiens, by a score of 3 to 2.

The building's most unique feature is the series of 13 bas-reliefs, located at eye level, on three sides of the structure. Executed by master stone-carver Louis Temporale Sr., the carvings represent the history of communications, especially the evolution of Canadian mail transportation and delivery. At the northeast corner we see depictions of human speech, log drumming, a runner carrying a message, and First Nations individuals communicating by smoke signal. The southeast corner, representing the period after European contact, depicts, a stagecoach, voyageurs paddling a canoe, and a dog sled. Concluding in the twentieth century, the southwest corner contains a letter carrier, an amphibious aircraft, a steamship, a clipper ship, a train, and a mail van (this final panel was moved to the indoor Heritage Exhibit).

ABOVE This 1992 photo of the east façade shows the Toronto Postal Delivery Building before it was transformed into the Air Canada Centre. The base of the building is black granite, with Queenston limestone above. The centre section of the east and south façade is Stripped Classical, with ribbed pilasters separating broad expanses of windows containing vertical glass panes. By contrast, the edges of the building are Streamlined Moderne, with slightly rounded corners and bold horizontal ribbon windows with horizontal panes.

Toronto Postal Delivery Building

ABOVE The bas-relief at the cornice is a repeating pattern of beavers nibbling on tree stumps, interspersed with maple leaves flanked by bulrushes.

RIGHT This roundel depicts a mighty moose standing in a swamp, surrounded by lily pads.

FAR RIGHT This roundel shows a V-shaped flock of Canada geese flying up from a lake at sunrise.

Dominion Public Building

45 Main Street East, Hamilton, Ontario

Hutton & Souter, 1934–36

The Dominion Public Building in Hamilton is one of the earliest large buildings erected under the Public Works Construction Act. One block long and six storeys high, it opened in September 1936. The ground floor contained a giant postal hall, while the upper floors housed Customs, Taxes, Immigration, Colonization, Relief, Pensions, National Health, and the RCMP.

ABOVE The left-hand end of the main façade's bas-relief portrays Western Canada. It features a fisherman bearing his catch, farmers planting and harvesting crops, and a First Nations trapper carrying pelts.

TOP RIGHT All the requisite features of a Stripped Classical edifice are present on the building's limestone exterior: a two-storey base with tall windows topped by a narrow cornice with simple geometric motifs; a four-storey shaft with vertically arranged windows separated by shallow fluted pilasters; and a frontispiece at the main entry containing a wide bas-relief panel of nationalist imagery near the roofline.

LEFT The main post office lobby is brightly lit from the tall ground-floor windows, supplemented by metal chandeliers suspended from the multi-coloured coffered ceiling. The floor is composed of four shades of marble. Above the wickets is an inlaid ceramic map of Canada.

Dominion Public Building

338 Keele Street, Toronto, Ontario
Craig & Madill, 1935

The area around the intersection of Dundas and Keele Streets in West Toronto began attracting foundries, mills, wire factories, and other industries in the 1870s due in part to cheaper land, affordable labour, and lower taxes, as well as the adjacent Canadian Pacific rail yards.

By the 1890s, the Village of West Toronto Junction became an official port of entry, which allowed businesses to clear goods locally rather than having to travel to the downtown Toronto port. As a result, there was an influx of businesses whose workforces included immigrants from England and Europe, plus Irish Catholics from crowded tenements elsewhere in the city. In 1909, the Village was amalgamated with the City of Toronto.

The Junction was home to the Ontario Stockyards for a half-century. For some time, it was the country's largest livestock market and the centre of the province's meat packing industry – helping Toronto gain its nickname of 'Hogtown.' With this industrial heft, it's not surprising that The Junction was selected as the site for a Dominion Public Building, housing a post office and customs department.

The building's architects worked in private practice, thus helping provide employment for architects and draftsmen. All the building's materials were sourced in Canada.

ABOVE LEFT On the protruding entrance blocks at either end, smooth bullnose segments aligned with the brick speed stripes interrupt the engaged fluted quarter-columns. The stylized dentils atop the entry block, and the cypher of the reigning monarch King George V, add a Stripped Classical touch to the façade.

TOP This two-storey, reinforced concrete structure is clad in grey-buff brick with stone trim. The speed stripes in the broad brick piers between the windows lend a Streamlined Moderne feel to the front façade.

ABOVE RIGHT As seen in this period photo, suspended circular light fixtures, geometric marble accents in the terrazzo floor, and a horizontal emphasis in the brushed chromium-plated bronze screens give the ground floor post office its Streamlined Moderne character.

Supreme Court of Canada

301 Wellington Street, Ottawa, Ontario

Ernest Cormier, 1938–44

After being formally established in 1875, the Supreme Court of Canada operated for decades out of the second floor of a converted stable and workshop near Parliament Hill. But a 1935 report said that the courthouse "should be condemned as being injurious to the health of the occupants and totally inadequate for the purpose for which it is used."

Recently re-elected Prime Minister Mackenzie King acted swiftly upon the report. He was influenced in part by the U.S. Supreme Court's recent move into prestigious new quarters on Capitol Hill; more importantly, he was keen to aesthetically improve Ottawa as a federal capital. Mackenzie King personally inspected and approved the site that had been previously identified for the new structure – set back from Wellington Street west of Parliament Hill, on a curved cliff overlooking the Ottawa River.

Although the architectural community wanted a competition, the Privy Council unilaterally awarded the project in June 1937 to Montreal-based architect and engineer Ernest Cormier. Eminently qualified for the project, Cormier had previously designed the Annex to the Palais de Justice in Montreal and the main pavilion of the Université de Montreal (see page 100), as well as having been a member of the Royal Canadian Academy since 1931.

The existing architectural language on Parliament Hill was 'picturesque,' drawn from such traditions as the English neo-Gothic style, the Second Empire style from France, Romanesque Revival, and finally the Château style (a melding of French Loire châteaux and Scottish manor houses, which New York architect Bruce Price pioneered at the Banff Springs Hotel in the late 1880s). But Cormier, trained at the *École des Beaux-Arts* in Paris, fully recognized the value of the Classical tradition as a means of signifying prestige and authority.

Although the Chief Justice approved the initial design, Mackenzie King considered it too modern and austere, comparing it, in his diary, to a factory. Cormier responded by making the massive copper roof more picturesque by adding three rows of dormer windows of decreasing size, together with

chimney stacks and turrets to the profile of the two light wells.

With the design now settled, construction of the steel-frame structure began in October 1938 and was completed in 1941. During the war, however, the building housed only employees of the National War Services, National Revenue, and National Defence, and did not finally welcome the Court until January 1946. It was soon discovered that the library was inconveniently located relative to the courtrooms, and was moved to the third floor that was originally intended for storage.

In subsequent years, Cormier designed the Court's furniture, which was not included in the initial commission.

ABOVE Like most of Ernest Cormier's work, the Supreme Court defies easy stylistic classification, although the main façade most closely follows Stripped Classical principles. Set well back from Wellington Street, a grand set of steps lead visitors up to the symmetrical twin entrances. The protruding side pavilions, housing the Federal Court and the Federal Court of Appeal, have fewer windows than the central taller block. Notice the strong shadow line that clearly separates the picturesque, steeply pitched copper roof from the finely detailed limestone façade.

Supreme Court of Canada

ABOVE LEFT Drawing upon his skills as an architect and engineer, Cormier created these elegant chandeliers for the Grand Entrance Hall using exposed fluorescent bulbs.

ABOVE RIGHT The Grand Entrance Hall – clothed in muted tones of Canadian and European marble – measures 32 by 17 metres, with a 12-metre coffered ceiling supported by giant Stripped Classical fluted columns and pilasters. The twin half-landing staircases accented by pink marble bannisters lead to a large balcony that is three steps below the floor level of the Supreme Court chamber. A bronze bas-relief of the original Supreme Court Building is mounted between the stairways.

TOP LEFT The theme of moving water – the primary means by which electricity was generated in this era – permeates the building's decoration. These zigzag 'sluices' are located atop the pilasters flanking the main entry.

TOP RIGHT The building's deeply recessed, two-storey entrance portal features a wavy glass-block wall above the doors. The brown metal spandrel panels on the façade above also contain wave motifs.

BOTTOM LEFT The wave motif continues inside on the metalwork of the main foyer doors, as well as in the foyer's decorative marble trim.

OPPOSITE The 18-storey, Zigzag-style tower, seen here before its conversion to the Princess Margaret Cancer Centre, stands between the Commission's earlier and later offices. The façade's multiple-plane stone piers separating the recessed windows curve up and over each step-back, creating a sense of uninterrupted verticality.

BC Power Commission Building

780 Blanshard Street, Victoria, British Columbia

B.C. Chief Architect Henry Whittaker, 1938–39

British Columbia's first electrical street lighting was switched on in Victoria in 1883, with electric streetcars arriving seven years later. At the turn of the century, passengers could pay 15 cents one way, or 25 cents return, to travel by electric railway from Victoria to Esquimalt.

As tungsten and nitrogen-gas-filled lamps became increasingly popular in the early 1920s, the privately owned British Columbia Electric Railway Company (BC Electric) stopped its 15-year practice of freely exchanging burned-out carbon filament lamps for new lamps. When Victoria and the Lower Mainland switched to driving on the right side of the road in January 1922, BC Electric received $370,000 from the province to adapt its streetcar tracks and rolling stock.

The Electric Power Act of 1945 created the British Columbia Power Commission, a publicly owned utility that existed alongside BC Electric until they were merged in 1962 to form the Crown corporation BC Hydro. The BC Power Commission's mandate was to consolidate the province's disparate generation and distribution facilities into a single system, and to stimulate industrialization and population growth by bringing electricity to the many smaller communities that were without power.

In 1945, the BC Power Commission moved into this Art Deco building, which was initially built for use as a hospital.

TOP Situated on a steeply sloping downtown site, the south-west-facing, four-storey façade features a full-height, multiple-plane frontispiece that boasts downward-pointing chevron spandrels and is topped by bands of vertical ridges. The incised speed-stripes on the façade of the first floor are paralleled by a horizontal band of vertical bevels spanning the façade above the third-floor windows. At least as far back as May 1992, the ground floor was painted a terra-cotta colour, with the upper floors off-white.

ABOVE RIGHT On account of its longevity, poured-in-place concrete was a favourite building material of architect Henry Whittaker. The formwork that molded the concrete could easily create a range of flat decoration such as the low-relief chevrons, vertical ridges, and half-discs seen here above the two-storey north façade's entrance.

Penticton Court House

100 Main Street, Penticton, British Columbia

B.C. Chief Architect Henry Whittaker, 1948–49

Sandwiched between hills and mountains at southern tip of Okanagan Lake, the town of Penticton was incorporated in 1908 with a population of 600. Two years later, it was chosen as headquarters for the new Kettle Valley Railway, which finally linked the Kootenay region to the east with the Pacific Ocean. The railway transported high-quality fruits from the Okanagan Valley to distant markets, while also establishing Penticton as a tourist destination. The town's population more than doubled in the five years it took to build the railway.

After World War II, Penticton grew further with the influx of a sizeable number of veterans, attracted by its semi-arid climate. By 1948, with local architect Robert Lyon as its mayor, Penticton finally became a city, and was selected as the site of a provincial courthouse. The new courthouse – located less than 200 metres from Okanagan Lake – also contained numerous offices, including the police and sheriff, plus public health, public works, education and agriculture departments.

At its opening official opening on a rainy Saturday March 19, 1949, the province's minister of public works described this building "as fine and modern as any you will find in Canada."

TOP The main block of the two-storey courthouse features Zigzag styling: windows arranged in vertical strips, separated by wavy-patterned spandrel panels.

LEFT Inside the circular foyer, the building splits into two wings, with matching staircases to the second floor. Notice the round columns with scalloped bottom detailing. The foyer floor contains a compass motif.

RIGHT The double-height, rounded corner entrance, flanked by narrow glass-block vertical window strips, is more Streamlined Moderne in style.

New Brunswick Electric Power Commission Building

527 King Street, Fredericton, New Brunswick

John L. Feeney (designer), 1949

While the building of small, privately owned coal-fired power plants in the larger centres of Moncton, Saint John, and Fredericton in the early 1880s marked the beginning of New Brunswick's electricity industry, power was slow to reach rural areas.

Recognizing the importance of electricity in enhancing his people's quality of life and growing the economy, Premier Walter E. Foster sought to create a government-owned electric company; the New Brunswick Electric Power Commission was born on April 24, 1920.

Despite the Depression, demand for electricity climbed during the 1930s, requiring additional generating capacity beyond the power generated by hydro dams. In response, a coal-fired plant was built near the mines at Minto, east of Fredericton. During World War II, the Commission added new generating capacity, distribution lines and substations, in part to meet the needs of the New Brunswick–based training facilities that the federal government provided for British Commonwealth Air Force personnel.

Initially, the Commission was based in Saint John, but due to a shortage of space and the desire to be closer to provincial government decision-makers, the head office moved to Fredericton in 1949. The design of its new building was handled by John L. Feeney, a civil engineer who joined the Commission in 1925. Although not a licensed architect, Feeney's skill in building design is very evident in the execution of the four-storey head office structure.

The Commission Building was not the only Stripped Classical structure in Fredericton; the 1951 Federal Building on nearby Queen Street is a hybrid of late Stripped Classical and early Modern design.

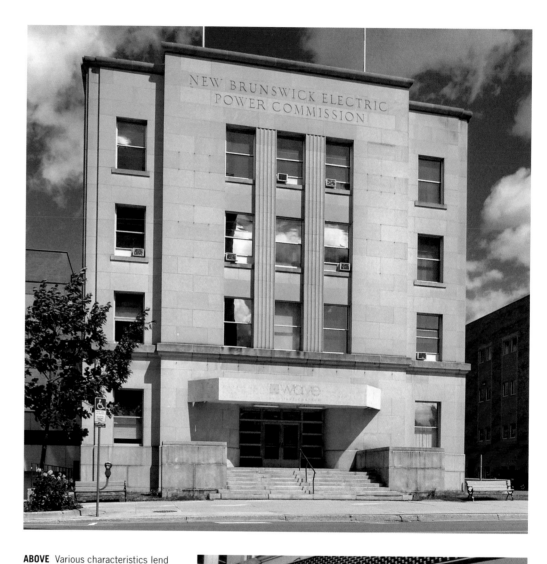

RIGHT The front entrance canopy had curved corners although its facing had been replaced in this 1994 photo. Notice the bullnose treatment of the walls flanking the brass front doors, and the horizontally proportioned sidelights.

ABOVE Various characteristics lend the four-storey façade its Stripped Classical styling. These include the slightly taller frontispiece containing two fluted pilasters and topped by the incised building name in a classic typeface, the multiple-plane treatment of the building corners, and the strong stone cornices atop the first and fourth floors.

Confederation Building

100 Prince Phillip Drive, St. John's, Newfoundland and Labrador
A.J.C. Paine; Lawson, Betts & Cash, (associates), 1956–60

Newfoundland's journey from being discovered by Viking explorer Leif Erikson to its 1949 entry into Canada was as rocky as the island's topography.

The island – together with Labrador, which it was awarded by Britain in 1927 – operated as its own Dominion, proud of its independence and dreaming of prosperity based on harvesting its natural resources of cod, minerals, and timber. But debt, distrust of its politicians, and the Depression forced it to relinquish its self-government in 1934.

During World War II, Britain granted the United States access to its naval bases in Newfoundland, producing an influx of money, jobs – and modern American ideas. Five American military bases arrived after the war. While Canada was becoming concerned about the possibility of Newfoundland joining the U.S., Britain was keen to cut its post-war spending.

In response, Britain convened a National Convention in 1946 to allow Newfoundlanders to decide their own fate, eventually insisting that union with Canada be among the options. It took two referendums in mid-1948 before a slim majority (52.3 percent) of Newfoundlanders voted for confederation with Canada. At midnight on March 31, 1949, Newfoundland officially became the 10th province; Joey Smallwood became its first premier two months later.

The House of Assembly sat in the 1850 neoclassical Colonial Building for a decade, but a new facility was desired that would bring all government departments together. The charismatic, forward-looking but autocratic Smallwood – a man who closely followed the trends of contemporary architecture – insisted on a monumental design that would reflect the province's new-found stature within Confederation.

With 675 rooms housing 1,200 employees, the $9-million Confederation Building featured a two-storey lobby that contained a giant mural presenting an allegorical representation of the province's history.

RIGHT The building combines Zigzag massing with Modern curtain-wall design; its vertically arranged windows are separated by plain, turquoise-coloured metal spandrels. At the building's entrance, a statue of explorer John Cabot looks out over Signal Hill and The Narrows.

ABOVE Perched high atop Confederation Hill – far away from downtown at the time – the symmetrical 11-storey building is nearly 200 metres wide and 64 metres high at its tallest. It is crowned with a steel-and-glass lantern, echoing the function of a coastal lighthouse from earlier days.

Municipal Government Buildings

Vancouver City Hall

453 West 12th Avenue, Vancouver, British Columbia
Townley & Matheson, 1935–36

Nearly 50 years after its incorporation in 1886, and despite its growth as a port thanks to the opening of the Panama Canal in 1914, the City of Vancouver still lacked a proper home for its municipal government. With unemployment reaching 20 percent by 1935 and the city's Golden Jubilee looming, newly elected mayor Gerry McGeer needed to act.

Instead of holding a design competition for the new city hall and thus boosting the fortunes of hard-pressed local architects, McGeer simply appointed the firm of Townley & Matheson. The mayor's choice may have been influenced by the many hunting and fishing trips he shared with his school-age friend Matheson, plus the fact that Townley's father had once served as mayor.

The location of the new building was also controversial, being sited on a hill some distance away from downtown, on the grounds of the former Strathcona Park. McGeer's vision – which has since proven true – was that the city would expand around the structure.

Beginning on January 3, 1936, hundreds of unemployed men went to work – without the benefit of motorized hand tools – and completed the $1-million structure in exactly 11 months.

A 2.5-metre statue of Captain George Vancouver, carved that year by the city's leading sculptor Charles Marega, announced the front entry to the building, which received its Schedule A Heritage Designation from the city in 1976.

ABOVE Thanks to its symmetrical plan, wedding-cake massing and windows treated as vertical strips, the 12-storey city hall is a fine example of Zigzag civic architecture.

RIGHT Like most Zigzag skyscrapers, the reinforced-concrete building with gray granite and sandstone cladding features a multi-storey entrance portal. Notice the contrasting spandrel panels above.

Dalhousie Town Hall

117 Hall Street, Dalhousie, New Brunswick

Frederick J. Bateman (designer), 1939

Incorporated as a town in 1905, Dalhousie is the northernmost community in the Province of New Brunswick, situated on the south shore of the Bay of Chaleur where the Restigouche River meets the ocean.

The area was first settled by Acadians, followed by a wave of Scottish immigrants from the Isle of Arran in the 1820s. The Scots gave the name 'Inch Arran Point' to the peninsula projecting out into Chaleur Bay, the term 'Inch' being Gaelic for point. The community gained its name in 1826, in honour of George Ramsay, the ninth Earl of Dalhousie, who was the governor of Upper and Lower Canada.

The arrival of the Intercolonial Railway in the late 1880s opened up the Restigouche region, and made Dalhousie an attractive vacation destination based on its temperate maritime climate. In the summer of 1887, one prominent visitor to the area was Prime Minister John A. Macdonald and his wife, Agnes.

The construction of the New Brunswick International Paper Company's mill in 1929 brought new employment opportunities. By 1939, the population had climbed to some 4,500 people; town clerk and engineer Fred Bateman was tasked with building a town hall. An expert in building with concrete, Bateman designed an attractive two-storey solid concrete structure that officially opened on July 24, 1939. The town hall is now recognized under the province's Historic Sites Protection Act.

Bateman was evidently knowledgeable about architectural styles, since he built his own three-storey fully concrete home – in Tudor Revival style – the following year.

ABOVE The two-storey block of the solid-concrete Dalhousie Town Hall features a central entrance recessed between two symmetrical wings. Its Stripped Classical features – including a protruding pediment above the front door flanked by fluted pilasters, and stylized dentils on the main and side façades – are complemented by Zigzag details such as the multiple-plane and step-back treatment of the recessed windows in the side wings.

Municipal Government Buildings

Penticton Municipal Hall

145 Main Street, Penticton, British Columbia
Robert M. Lyon, 1940 (demolished mid-1960s)

Described in a headline as "Modernistic Architecture Combined With Efficiency" in an October 31, 1940 story in *The Penticton Herald*, the town's new Municipal Hall was opened that month without a formal ceremony, since the council felt this would not be appropriate in wartime.

The structure was designed by the talented and prolific local architect, Robert Lyon, who would go on to become mayor when Penticton was incorporated as a city in 1948.

The building housed Penticton's civic offices, as well as the town library with its own entrance. According to the newspaper article, "Every possible convenience for the promotion of efficiency in the civic organization has been included in the new building. At the same time, construction costs were kept to a minimum, the Council and the architect endeavoring to avoid all 'frills'."

Climbing the three curved stairs at the east-facing front door, visitors passed through the modest vestibule before entering the public space with its sturdy maple floors and a partial skylight. They conducted their business with the town's general office at a counter with a 'modernistic' screen that featured large chromium bars. Opposite the office was the council chamber, looking out onto Main Street; it was "a business-like room that has adequate space for the Council and any delegations that may, in future times, wait upon the civic leaders." In the centre were two vaults for storing municipal books, records, and blueprints, and behind them, the general engineering area with private offices for an engineer and draftsman.

A relief office, located at the rear of the building, was equipped with its own ante-room and private entrance "to eliminate any embarrassment on the part of the less fortunate citizens of the community."

The library – to the south of the civic offices and set back from the main façade – was built to house 7,000 volumes, based on the standing practice of removing out-of-date books. The librarian's desk was strategically situated to oversee the enclosed reading room as well as rows of bookshelves.

The demolition of this distinctive Streamlined Moderne building less than three decades after it was built is indeed a sad loss.

ABOVE Rounded corners and horizontal stripes featured prominently on the now-demolished municipal hall. The main entrance is announced by a half-cylinder that protruded above the rest of the façade and prominently bore the building's name and year in period lettering. To the left is the town's library. The stucco façade combined an English texture (pebbled finish) on the upper areas with smooth trowelled finish below, and was painted in a buff colour. "The façade will present a striking appearance, yet will harmonize well with the park-like surroundings," noted the local newspaper.

LIFE IN THE
COMMUNITY

The Art Deco buildings in this chapter may be classified as institutional or civic structures – places where Canadians expanded their knowledge, congregated for worship, regained their health, and gathered for social occasions. The final group of buildings may be considered 'infrastructure' – feats of civil engineering that made possible the public services needed for daily life.

Police and Fire Station No. 10

1684 Maisonneuve Boulevard West, Montreal, Quebec

Shorey & Ritchie, 1931

It was not uncommon in 1930s Montreal to build structures that housed both police stations and fire stations. While several of its peers elsewhere in the city were constructed of brick and cut stone, Station No. 10 was an all-stone affair. Like other fire stations of its time, a tall hose-drying tower figured prominently in the building's massing.

The two functions occupied adjoining sides of the building: the front door of the police station faced northwest onto Maisonneuve Boulevard (then known as St. Luke Street), while the fire station's three engine bays opened onto St. Matthew Street. Since the building was constructed in a more anglophone neighbourhood, the words 'Police Station' and 'Fire Station' are carved in English. The building was honoured in 1931 with a 'First Award' in the Public Buildings category by the Royal Architectural Institute of Canada.

Today, a breakfast establishment has replaced the police station, while Fire Station No. 10 is still in operation.

ABOVE LEFT The top of the hose-drying tower features overlapping chevron motifs interspersed with vertical bands of floral scrolls, all beneath a crown of vertical scalloped fluting. The cutouts in the opening below allowed the fire hoses to dry out.

TOP Aside from the Police Station entrance doors, the two primary façades of the three-storey main block are essentially identical. Enlivening the ground floor are alternating stripes of rougher stone; the upper two floors are smooth. Two tall recessed windows on each façade contain a mix of horizontally proportioned and square glass panes. The hose-drying tower stands at the rear of the building.

ABOVE The boats in the decorative panel above the front door allude to Montreal's status as an urban port. The classic Art Deco floral scroll and chevron motifs in the background are echoed in the carved-stone banding above the first floor.

Firehall No. 12
840 Gerrard Street East, Toronto, Ontario
City of Toronto Architect, 1932

Toronto's Gerrard Street was named after Samuel Gerrard, an Anglo-Irish businessman who served as the second president of the Bank of Montreal, and from 1838 to 1841, as a member of the Special Council of Lower Canada.

In 1932, Firehall No. 12 was built just west of the railway bridge over Gerrard Street that carried freight and passengers from Union Station to points east. Today, the neighbourhood is considered east Riverdale.

In addition to three fire truck bays – instead of the usual two – the firehall's ground floor housed a sitting room at the rear; along the east side was a one-storey hose room and washroom. The second floor contained 11 bedrooms, plus a 'lavatory' separated from a 'wash room' that contained three sinks and two enclosed bathtubs.

Designed by the City of Toronto Architect's office with the primary design handled by Stanley T.J. Fryer, Firehall No. 12 incorporates the distinctive combination of light-buff brick and Queenston limestone with copper trim found in several police stations and other civic buildings created by the City Architect's office during this period.

ABOVE A taller stone frontispiece dominates the two-storey, symmetrical yellow brick façade. Notice the subtle differences in the proportions of the panes in the second-floor windows.

RIGHT The decorative highlight of the building is the bas-relief carving atop the frontispiece that extends above the roofline. A period journal described the building's top as "terminating in a feature carved in a free symbolism of flames and lightning shooting out of a half circle."

LEFT Fryer's masterful use of multiple planes with a mix of horizontal and vertical lines creates bold shadows on the façade. Stylistically, the building combines Zigzag and Streamlined Moderne elements.

Libraries and Museums

Runnymede Public Library

2178 Bloor Street West, Toronto, Ontario

John M. Lyle, 1929

An 1882 Act of the Ontario legislature created the institution of free libraries, through which a library was funded by local taxes rather than subscription fees. In the early years of the twentieth century, Scottish-American philanthropist Andrew Carnegie, who made his fortune in the steel industry, paid for the construction of 10 Carnegie libraries in Toronto, and a total of 125 library buildings across Canada. These often-imposing structures featured a prominent front entry reached by a set of steps, symbolizing the user's 'elevation' through learning.

In the post-Carnegie period of the 1920s, six new branches were constructed, and five new library associations formed. At the end of the decade, it was decided that the Runnymede neighbourhood needed its own library branch.

A 1929 Canadian architectural journal article noted that the function of a branch library had evolved from being a place to store books to being "the intellectual home of the community." This helps explain why architect John M. Lyle's brief from the Toronto Library Board was to design a building whose character was both domestic and semi-public.

Functionally, Lyle responded by creating a two-storey 'house.' The ground floor served adults, with book stacks located against the walls and an open reading space in the middle. Boys and girls used a side entrance from Glendonwynne Road to reach their own reading room on the second floor.

The Runnymede branch was designed when Lyle was focused on incorporating Canadian-inspired motifs in his work. He employed bell-curved eaves on the branch's steeply pitched, black slate roofs to evoke French Canada, and framed its front entrance with stone totem poles inspired by West Coast First Nations. Furthermore, he favoured local materials, including rough-textured limestone from the nearby Credit Valley for the exterior walls.

While its overall form is not Art Deco, the building's decorative elements make it worthy of inclusion in this book. Renovations to the library completed in 2005 have added more space without detracting from its original character.

ABOVE Above the children's entrance is a bas-relief carving of a First Nations man's face.

RIGHT The front entrance, recessed into a smooth-stone frontispiece, is flanked by two carved-stone totem poles depicting a raven, beaver, and bear. Above the doors, notice the Deco-styled lamp of knowledge motif and the band of chevrons.

BOTTOM RIGHT The double-hung ground floor and dormer windows help create the impression of a large house – appropriate since the library was situated in a residential neighbourhood.

Administration Building, Montreal Botanical Garden

4101 Sherbrooke Street East, Montreal, Quebec
Lucien Kéroack, 1932–37

After years of campaigning by Christian Brother Marie-Victorin, the Montreal Botanical Garden finally came into being in 1931, when Mayor Camillien Houde agreed to support the project as one of the city's job-creation initiatives.

Renowned horticulturalist and botanist Henry Teuscher drafted the first plan for the property; he was later officially appointed Superintendent and Chief Horticulturalist.

In 2008, the Botanical Garden was designated a National Historic Site of Canada. Today, it boasts 30 thematic gardens, 10 exhibition greenhouses, and 22,000 different plant species and cultivars, making it one of the world's largest and most spectacular botanical gardens.

The Administration Building was designed by Lucien Kéroack and built between 1932 and 1937. While its symmetrical plan and sense of monumentality reflect the influence of the earlier *Beaux-Arts* style, its architectural detailing and bas-relief decoration, by Montreal sculptor Henri Hébert, are firmly Art Deco.

TOP LEFT The stone front entrance features multiple planes with step-back massing. A carved panel above the front door depicts two young girls pulling petals from a daisy, symbolizing the scientific quest for truth. Inside the entrance foyer, the inlaid floor features stylized lilies, while the walls list the names of 16 well-known botanists.

TOP RIGHT Symmetrical brick wings that terminate in taller pavilions with copper roofs flank the building's central stone block. Accenting the front entrance is a long stepped fountain that was added in 1937. The front of the fountain contains an octagonal bas-relief of Saturn, the Roman god associated with bounty and agriculture, carved by Italian-born sculptor Joseph Guardo.

BOTTOM RIGHT In this end pavilion, the multiple planes of brickwork framing the windows, together with the subtly decorated spandrel panels, create a sense of verticality that contrasts with the horizontal stone banding at various levels. The two terracotta bas-reliefs at the top depict a habitant man collecting maple sap, and a moose eating water lilies. The two carved roundels above the first floor feature pine cones and maple leaves.

Administration Building, Montreal Botanical Garden

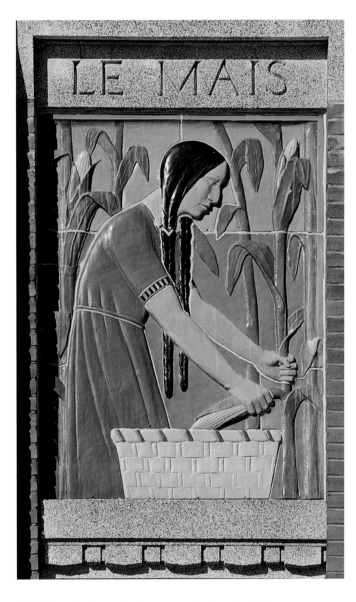

ABOVE These two terracotta bas-relief panels were created by Montreal sculptor Henri Hébert. The left panel – whose carved inscription translates as 'corn' – depicts a First Nations woman crushing corn. The right panel – 'birch' – shows a First Nations hunter in a birchbark canoe.

Spring Garden Road Memorial Library Building

5381 Spring Garden Road, Halifax, Nova Scotia

Leslie Raymond Fairn, 1949

With Halifax growing in the early years of the twentieth century, discussions arose about the need for a new library. After World War II was over, a committee of businessmen, politicians, and local citizens agreed that the most fitting way to honour the Haligonians who lost their lives in the two world wars was in the form of a library. It was felt that a statue or monument could not do justice to their memory, but that a library – which fostered learning and growth – would better represent the ideals of freedom for which the war was fought.

The cornerstone of the new building was laid on Remembrance Day 1949, with the doors of the 3,500-square-metre structure opening on November 12, 1951.

The memorial items featured in the library – assembled with the assistance of the Canadian Legion, the Silver Cross Women of Canada, and the Imperial Order Daughters of the Empire (IODE) – included flags, plaques, a replica of the Silver Cross, and two Books of Remembrance listing the names of the fallen (one for each war).

In 2014, the downtown library was moved to a bold new building across the street. After much debate, the memorial artifacts from the 1949 building were respectfully moved to the new Central Library or to the Maritime Command Museum. The future of the Memorial Library building, owned by the Halifax Regional Municipality, remains unclear.

ABOVE The flattened, temple-front stone façade with fluted pilasters, geometrically decorated spandrel panels, and the unadorned roundels in the frieze all contribute to the building's Stripped Classical styling. Both ends of the main block of the T-shaped structure feature curved protruding bays. Above the front entrance is a bas-relief carving of the Halifax coat of arms of the day, bearing the motto 'E Mari Merces' (Wealth from the Sea).

Houses of Worship

Ste. Clare Roman Catholic Church

166 Tecumseh Road West, Windsor, Ontario

Albert James Lothian, 1930

After its incorporation in 1892, the city of Windsor experienced rapid growth from the flourishing automotive industry, with its population increasing five-fold in just 20 years. Ste. Clare Roman Catholic Church was erected in 1930–31 to serve the city's growing community of Italian and French Catholics.

Six decades later, the church was in danger of demolition due to a decline in attendance and the subsequent consolidation of parishes. Ultimately, the building was purchased by a group of Maronite Catholics, a branch of the Eastern Catholic Church that was named in honour of the seventh-century saint, John Maron. This group of predominantly Lebanese Canadians renamed the church St. Peter's Maronite Church.

Within a year of its purchase, the building had been granted a Municipal Heritage Designation, which recognized its architectural and historical value under the Ontario Heritage Act. The church remains an integral part of the Windsor Maronite community.

The building's architect, Albert J. Lothian, was responsible for all design elements, from the elaborate spire to the window sconces, fine oak pews, and painted Stations of the Cross.

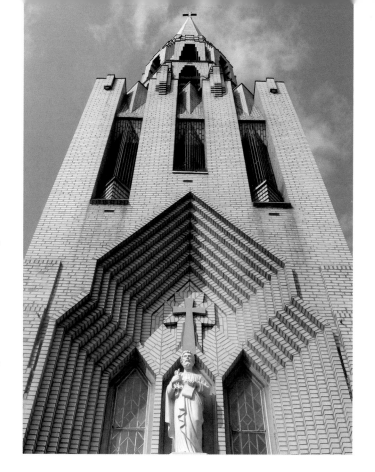

RIGHT This view directly up the main spire showcases architect Albert J. Lothian's mastery in creating three-dimensional ecclesiastical forms and spaces working only with brick. Non-figural stained-glass windows bring light into the interior of the tower.

BOTTOM RIGHT This side view of the buff-brick church reveals the non-traditional, elliptical-shaped sanctuary to the left, plus the towering spire over the main entrance that is capped with an aluminum-clad roof and cross. Notice the prevalence of step-shaped openings in the tower, and the multitude of triangular and linear vertical patterns in the brickwork throughout the façade.

Ste. Philomena of Rosemont Roman Catholic Church

2851 Masson Street, Montreal, Quebec

Joseph Eglide Cesaire Daoust, 1932–33

In 1903, real estate developer Ucal Henri Dandurand partnered with Herbert Samuel Holt, president of Montreal Light, Heat & Power, to establish the Rosemont Land Improvement Company. (The area was named Rosemont, in honour of Rose Phillips, Dandurand's 71-year-old Scottish mother.) The company subdivided the farmland it had purchased north of the Canadian Pacific Railway's Angus manufacturing and repair shops, with the aim of selling residential lots to CPR workers. Dandurand uniquely offered his purchasers the opportunity to pay via installments for their property. When the City of Montreal annexed the village of Rosemont in 1906, Dandurand and Holt were pleased, since it saved them from having to pay infrastructure costs for their new subdivision.

To serve this working-class community, the archbishop of Montreal established the Ste. Philomena Rosemont parish in 1905, named after the woman whose husband had donated land on Masson Street for the chapel. (The 'original' Philomena was a fourth-century teenage virgin martyr who reportedly possessed miraculous curative powers.)

By this time, Masson Street boasted a tram, and was fast becoming an active business centre serving the wave of Italian immigrants. As a result, the first chapel became too small, and a larger building was required; Montreal-born architect Joseph Eglide Cesaire Daoust was chosen to design the new church. This magnificent Art Deco structure was completed in two stages: the basement in 1922–23, and the remainder in 1932–33. The church was consecrated in 1933; its original painted steeple was removed in 1949.

In 1961, when the Vatican ruled that Philomena was not, in fact, a saint, the church was renamed St-Esprit de Rosemont. It was designated a Heritage Site by the City of Montreal in 1991.

The church contains a Casavant Frères organ; Italian-born Montrealer Guido Nincheri designed its stained-glass windows. The interior was the work of Montreal-born Toussait-Xénophon Renaud.

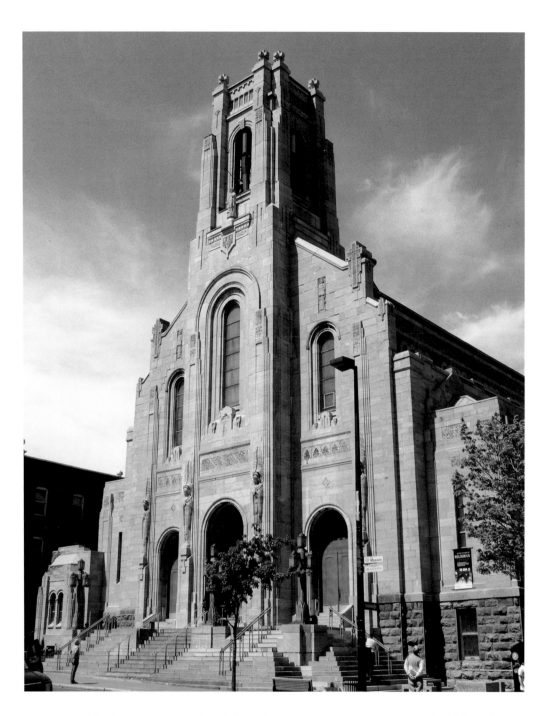

ABOVE Although the limestone church has a Latin cross floor plan and displays massing more reflective of conventional Gothic Revival styling, it possesses a number of Zigzag features. These include the flattened treatment of the decorative details, and the multiple-plane, step-back treatment of the front façade's pilasters.

Ste. Philomena of Rosemont Roman Catholic Church

FAR RIGHT A pair of bronze torchères that feature splendid geometric decoration at the base and brackets grace the church's exterior. Notice the bas-relief limestone angels with their sizeable wings flanking the entrance.

RIGHT Exquisite step-back massing and multiple-plane detailing adorn the church's façade. The carved decorative panels combine Deco floral motifs with Christian symbols.

BOTTOM RIGHT Black, green, and beige vinyl floor tiles are arranged in variations of a cross-shaped pattern.

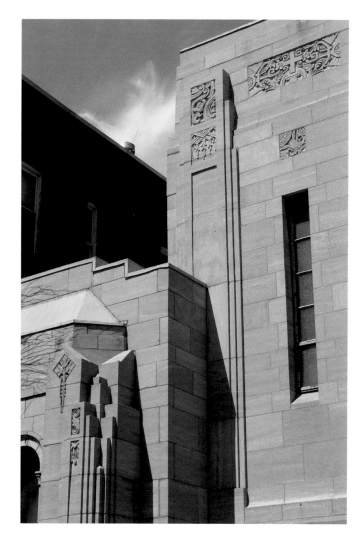

Houses of Worship

TOP LEFT The frosted-glass sconces between the wall arches boast a bold pyramidal pattern.

LEFT A wonderful, multi-sided, frosted-glass chandelier hangs from a multiple-plane cross in the sanctuary.

BOTTOM LEFT The detailing on the wooden altar chairs blends such trademark Zigzag motifs as sunbursts and a step-back profile beneath the seats.

St. James' Anglican Church

303 East Cordova Street, Vancouver, British Columbia

Adrian Gilbert Scott; Sharp & Thompson (associates), 1935–37

So intense was Vancouver's Great Fire of 1886 that it melted the bell of the original 1881 St. James' Church, located on a nearby site; the resulting solid puddle of metal was put on display in the Museum of Vancouver. Today's church, situated on land donated by the Canadian Pacific Railway, was the second house of worship built at the present location.

Fred Townley – a partner in the successful Vancouver architectural firm of Townley & Matheson – had sung in St. James' choir as a boy. Although he offered to design the current building for free, the church fathers selected London-based architect Adrian Gilbert Scott, who was a distant relative of the Rector, Reverend Canon Wilberforce Cooper. (Scott – who never actually visited Vancouver – was the grandson of nineteenth-century British architect Sir George Gilbert Scott, who was widely known for his Gothic Revival churches and cathedrals.) When Townley was subsequently asked to supervise the construction of Scott's building without pay, he was so offended that he never attended church again.

Architect Scott would have preferred brick, but monolithic reinforced concrete was chosen instead. Depression economics dictated a flat ceiling rather than a more dramatic vaulted ceiling beneath the central bell tower.

The completed building was consecrated in 1938; today, it actively serves and supports its local community in accordance with its Anglo-Catholic values.

TOP Located on a tight corner lot in downtown Vancouver's East Side, St. James' is a modern adaptation of Byzantine and Gothic design principles. A broad set of steps on the bevelled southwest corner lead up to the main entrance, accented by a series of simple recessed frames in the concrete wall. The cruciform floor plan contains transepts of unequal length, with the rear of the nave illuminated by three tall lancet windows.

LEFT This view of the slate-covered octagonal tower highlights the decorative treatment on the parapet. The repeating 45-degree protrusions of alternating heights echo medieval castle crenellations and reflect the overall angled geometry of the building. The church's façade was left unpainted until 1972.

Royal Oak Crematorium Chapel

4673 Falaise Drive, Victoria, British Columbia
C. Elwood Watkins, 1937

In 1918, the councils of Victoria, Saanich, Oak Bay, and Esquimalt began working together to find a location for a new cemetery for the region. Esquimalt and Oak Bay left the search before a site was chosen, but Victoria and Saanich carried on, finally purchasing a 32-hectare farm with views of Juan de Fuca Strait. The property's rolling hills and forests ensured that future burial plots would enjoy privacy from the major roadway to the west and the residential neighbourhood to the east.

The Royal Oak Burial Park opened on November 28, 1923, with its first burial taking place two days later. To this day, it operates as a non-profit cemetery, managed by a board of trustees established by the two municipalities.

When B.C. premier 'Honest' John Oliver died in August 1927, the funeral procession from the Parliament Buildings to Royal Oak included such luminaries as Lieutenant-Governor Robert Randolph Bruce, representatives of all levels of government, foreign consuls, naval and military officers, war veterans, and members of the public.

In spite of the Depression, the cemetery board recognized the need for a chapel and crematorium, spending $16,000 on its construction in 1937. Located close to the burial park's entrance, the stucco-covered masonry building has housed burial ceremonies for eight decades. Behind the entrance vestibule, the chapel rises to a double-height volume with clerestory windows, flanked on three sides by single-storey spaces.

Sixty years later, the chapel and crematorium building was recognized as a Historic Place of British Columbia; it is listed on the Saanich Heritage Registry on account of its significant community heritage value. Royal Oak is Vancouver Island's only burial park possessing a crematorium.

To meet the community's evolving needs, Royal Oak purchased land north of the original farm, added a memorial spot for cremated remains, built a mausoleum, and established a 'green' burial zone that is left in a natural state and maintained without pesticides.

ABOVE The building's front façade offers a pleasing balance of Zigzag and Streamlined Moderne elements. Protruding vertical piers extending slightly above the parapet on both the front façade and on the chimney at the rear enhance the impression of height, as do the flush panels with vertical ribbing, presented in a contrasting colour, that are found throughout the façade. The multiple planes on the piers framing the entrance doors match the step-back treatment atop the vestibule.

Benedictine Abbey of Saint Benoît-du-Lac

Overlooking Lake Memphremagog, near Mansonville, Quebec

Father Paul Bellot; Felix Racicot and Father Claude-Marie Côté (associates), 1939–41

Benedict of Nursia, the sixth-century patron saint of Europe and of students, is widely recognized for the moderate tone of his 'Rule of St. Benedict' that governed the communal life of monks.

The Benedictine monks of St. Wandrille, who were exiled from France in 1901 as a result of anticlerical laws, first moved to Belgium but ultimately settled in Canada in 1912, purchasing a hillside farm overlooking Lake Memphremagog in the Eastern Townships of Quebec. Over the next two decades – despite being cut off from St. Wandrille due to World War I, and the accidental drowning in 1914 of their founding Father – the community of Saint Benoît-du-Lac endured and expanded, finally gaining its autonomy in 1935.

Meanwhile, at the request of two of his Quebec followers, Paris-born architect Father Paul Bellot had delivered – in 1934 in Montreal, Quebec City, and Sherbrooke – a series of 19 lectures on art and architecture. Bellot, who studied at the *École des Beaux-Arts* in Paris and had joined a Benedictine order in 1904, had already designed numerous European churches and abbeys.

Bellot believed that the structure of a building should be exposed instead of hidden, and that decorative details should arise from the structure itself. He introduced to Quebec what some called the 'Dom Bellot Style' that featured roofs supported by multiple parabolic arches (that early on were constructed of bricks in contrasting colours), plus other geometric decoration.

By 1938, the monks at Saint Benoît-du-Lac decided to build their own monastery, and asked Father Bellot to design it. He returned to Canada to prepare the plans for this structure (and also the concrete shell dome of St. Joseph's Oratory in Montreal). Bellot died of cancer three years after the monastery was opened in 1941, and was buried on the property. In 1952 the monastery was elevated to the status of Abbey.

Today, about 40 monks live at the Abbey, separated from the everyday world, seeking and serving God. Outsiders are welcome to visit and join in reciting Gregorian chants, some of which date back more than 1,000 years.

ABOVE The Benedictine Abbey overlooking Lac Memphremagog displays a modern update of Gothic and Romanesque forms. It features simplified pointed-arch windows and flattened buttresses, and employs a more picturesque pentagonal courtyard rather than the traditional quadrangular format. Its structure is reinforced concrete, faced in local white granite.

RIGHT The soft colours and high ceiling supported by exposed structural ribs make this room ideal for quiet contemplation. Notice the repeating pattern of terracotta and beige brick above the tripartite pointed-top windows and atop the fireplace.

LEFT This sensational cloister contains the key features of the 'Dom Bellot Style': clear expression of the corbelled parabolic structural arches; bold, earth-tone geometric patterns in the glazed floor tiles; and multicoloured banding in the brick walls and recessed window arches.

Our Lady of the Assumption Cathedral

226 St. George Street, Moncton, New Brunswick

Louis-Napoléon Audet, 1939–40

In an event known as the Great Expulsion, some 11,500 Acadians – descendants of seventeenth-century French colonists – were driven out of Canada's Maritime provinces between 1755 and 1764 by the ruling British. Since then, Acadians have returned to New Brunswick and other provinces, determined to overcome past discrimination and celebrate their distinctive culture, Catholic religion, language, and other traditions.

When Moncton's Acadian community needed a place of worship in the 1930s, it was natural that their new cathedral would honour their patron saint (Saint Mary, Our Lady of the Assumption).

Our Lady of the Assumption Cathedral was begun in 1939 and completed in record time a year later. Situated a few blocks from the shore of the Petitcodiac River, it was compared to Notre-Dame Cathedral on the banks of the Seine in Paris. Its 70-metre tower dominated the city's skyline until the early 1970s.

The building's Sherbrooke, Quebec–based architect, Louis-Napoléon Audet, had been designing cathedrals for three decades; its four white-marble interior statues and two mosaics were created by Edmundston, N.B. – born Claude Roussel, who was recognized as a pioneer of Acadian sculpture.

Improvements made in 1955 – in celebration of the bicentennial of the Acadian Deportation – included the installation of a Casavant Frères pipe organ in the gallery, and permanent church pews. Pope John Paul II paid a visit to the Cathedral in 1984.

ABOVE The building is a modernized version of the standard Gothic Revival cathedral, with a cruciform footprint and pointed-arch windows. Clerestory windows on three sides illuminate the high, smooth vaulted ceiling above the olive sandstone walls.

TOP RIGHT The ashlar treatment of the towering 70-metre sandstone steeple is accented on all sides by protruding smooth-stone crosses with pointed arch tops and rectangular punched openings. Notice the Zigzag-style step-back massing of the lower walls, and how the vertical window band flanked by copper vents emphasizes the Cathedral's height.

BOTTOM RIGHT The detailing of this interior sandstone pilaster capital is distinctly non-ecclesiastical; it depicts a modern airplane flying over waves, framed between Art Deco floral spirals.

St. Mary's Cathedral

219 – 18th Avenue S.W., Calgary, Alberta

Maxwell Bates, 1954–57

The first St. Mary's Church was completed in 1899 and consecrated as St. Mary's Cathedral in 1913. A 1,000-seat sandstone structure with twin-domed towers, it is believed that delays in its construction caused structural weaknesses that necessitated its demolition in 1955.

Its replacement – built with a steel and reinforced concrete skeleton and sheathed in light-coloured brick – was completed in 1957 at a cost of $1 million.

This work was the crowning achievement of its architect, Maxwell Bates, who – although he had apprenticed with his architect father in Calgary and had served in the 1930s as chief assistant to a prominent Gothic Revival restoration architect in London, England – was actually better known as an author, poet, painter, and printmaker. Bates invested countless hours in the design of his masterwork, exhaustively studying church symbolism and ultimately producing 400 drawings of interior details. The 'Madonna with Child' sculpture that graces the front entrance was created by Alberta ceramacist, painter, and sculptor Luke Lindoe.

Despite interior alterations in 1989, the Cathedral retains many of its original features.

ABOVE The Cathedral's overall form, slender windows, and prominent tower are Gothic Revival, but the architectural treatment of its buff-brick skin reflects its modernity.

TOP RIGHT Alberta sculptor Luke Lindoe's 'Madonna with Child' cast-concrete sculpture over the front entrance is nearly seven metres in height and weighs more than six tons. He also designed the façade's cast-stone decorative panels.

BOTTOM RIGHT The step-back massing and multiple planes make the 40-metre bell tower a masterpiece of Zigzag styling. Inside the open brick crown are four bells, cast in France, that were saved from the first church.

Educational Buildings

Main Pavilion, University of Montreal

2900 Edouard-Montpetit Boulevard, Montreal, Quebec

Ernest Cormier, 1924–43

Fewer than 100 students were enrolled at the University of Montreal – then a branch of Laval University in Quebec – when it opened in 1878. When it moved to new premises on Saint-Denis Street in Montreal in 1905, all of its faculties were consolidated in one building. The university gained its independence from Laval in 1919.

Fires in 1919 and 1922 that damaged the Saint-Denis building led the respected francophone institution to build a new campus on a sizeable site, donated by the City of Montreal, that was located on the northwest slope of Mount Royal. The university's executive committee rejected the demand from Quebec's Association of Architects for a competition, and instead contracted Montreal's talented and visionary 'architect and engineer-builder' Ernest Cormier to draw up plans.

Cormier's first sketches were prepared in 1924; in January 1928, he unveiled a cardboard architectural model of the building. Excavation commenced that May but was suspended in 1931 for a decade. The building was finally completed in 1943 and inaugurated on June 3, Ascension Day.

The giant complex stretches more than 270 metres from end to end, and is laid out according to *Beaux-Arts* planning principles. Six projecting wings are linked together and joined in the centre, framing the Courtyard of Honour. Classrooms occupy the northwesterly wings, while a teaching hospital briefly filled the southeastern wings. In a break with tradition for a Catholic institution, the chapel was not positioned in the centre of the building, but rather to the rear of the hospital wing. The central administrative building contains offices, lecture halls, a sizeable auditorium, and the library. It is crowned by a 75-metre-tall tower symbolizing the university's role as a beacon of higher learning, which later housed the library stacks.

Describing the style of the Main Pavilion as simply Art Deco does a disservice to its sophisticated composition and architectural treatment. Cormier drew upon well-published international architectural precedents for various elements: the tower echoed Helsinki's railway station and Nebraska's State Capitol, while the chapel's stepped profile took inspiration from the Grundtvig Church in Copenhagen. Yet there are indeed

elements of Art Deco in the design. The overall step-back massing and multiple planes found throughout the building, as well as the arrangement of the classroom pavilion's windows in recessed vertical strips, obey Zigzag principles; the treatment of the opposite wing's windows as flush horizontal bands that wrap around the corners is more in keeping with Streamlined Moderne.

For economic, practical and aesthetic reasons, the building's façade is made of brick rather than stone. Specifically, Cormier used buff-coloured glazed brick from Ohio, citing its ability to "give the walls a richer appearance" and enhance the effects of light and shadow.

Today, the Main Pavilion remains a landmark on the city's skyline, with a stylized view of the tower serving as the institution's logo.

ABOVE This contemporary aerial photo showcases the 277-metre length of the Main Pavilion with its six linked projecting wings. When completed in 1943, the building stood alone on the campus property on the northwest face of Mount Royal.

LEFT The roofline of the main pavilion, seen here from the rear, is highlighted by three elements. The iconic central tower – whose height is accentuated by its elongated vertical window strips and round dome – rises 75 metres from the ground. To the extreme left is the sloped roof of the chapel; the pyramidal form on the right marks the amphitheatre. Directly to the rear of the tower is the auditorium, with its gently curving rear wall and stepped curved roof.

Main Pavilion, University of Montreal

TOP RIGHT The interior of the auditorium is a study in crisp geometry. The multiple recesses of the curved ceiling – gently illuminated by cove lighting – correspond with the diminishing height and width of the rectangular arch framing the slightly convex stage.

RIGHT The oxidized copper canopies over the three warm-coloured, wooden main entry doors each feature a small dome. Notice the engaged quarter-columns with convex fluting. The hexagonal shape of the transom windows is replicated, in simplified form, in Cormier's 1948 design for St. Michael's College School in Toronto.

BOTTOM RIGHT At the centre of the entrance hall, a ring of faceted marble columns encircling a recessed ceiling announces the doors to the library. In a nod to Cormier's respect for modern technology, the chandeliers consist of exposed fluorescent tubes.

Cherrier Roman Catholic School

811 Cherrier Street, Montreal, Quebec
C.A. Eugene Larose, 1931

The history of education in Quebec is inexorably linked with religion. Canada's 1867 Constitution enshrined education as a provincial responsibility, and decreed that in Quebec, Protestants and Catholics would have separate schools, run by their own school boards. The Catholic clergy insisted that it – not the provincial government – was best suited to teaching young people, and was able to maintain this power until the education system was secularized as part of the Quiet Revolution in the 1960s.

Some years ago, Cherrier Roman Catholic School was decommissioned as a Catholic school, and is presently home to a specialty educational facility for teenagers with learning and behavioural disabilities.

ABOVE This close-up of the front façade highlights the building's remarkable brick detailing. The right-hand corner pier is topped by a triangular motif of protruding bricks. On the central pier, the slightly bevelled top section transitions into a stack of increasingly recessed bricks that ultimately become vertical ribs of varying widths.

TOP This side view of the building was shot in 1989, when it was still operating as Cherrier School. A range of vertical elements makes the structure appear taller than its three storeys. Notice the original double-hung windows, and the copper lettering above the door.

LEFT The edges of the protruding brick pilasters at the main entrance feature vertical ribbons of projecting bricks that lead the eye upward. The building's Zigzag character is further reinforced by the chevrons found on the lintels above the upper-floor windows and the vertical banding in the brick spandrels. This contemporary photo shows how the windows have been updated.

Merritton High School

10 Seymour Avenue, St. Catharines, Ontario

Lionel Ashton Hesson, 1934–35

The inspiration for a canal to bypass the Niagara River came to William Hamilton Merritt while conducting constant patrols of the river as part of a cavalry unit during the War of 1812. After the war, Merritt – whose father had fought in the War of Independence as a United Empire Loyalist – operated a sawmill and grist mill on Twelve Mile Creek, about 20 kilometres east of the Niagara River. He was particularly frustrated by the creek's fluctuating low water levels during peak grain-harvesting season in late summer, and sought to remedy this by diverting water from Chippawa Creek (today's Welland River, flowing north into the Niagara River).

That effort evolved into the first Welland Canal, which was built between 1824 and 1829 by the Welland Canal Company; the entrepreneurial Merritt served as its financial agent. That canal passed through a community originally known as Welland City, which gained the name Merrittsville in 1844 in honour of Merritt's contribution to the community's growth. The community – located on the west side of today's (fourth) Welland Canal – was later renamed Merritton before being absorbed, in 1961, as a council ward of today's St. Catharines. Nevertheless, Merritton remains a distinct community that is proud of its history and its connection to the canal.

Merritton High School, built in 1934–35 with subsequent additions, served the community admirably until its closure in 1999. The building became a private boarding school for 13 years before suddenly ceasing operations; it reopened in April 2015 as a different private school.

TOP The stone frontispiece and adjoining fluted pilasters add verticality to the façade. Various decorative details within the frontispiece – including the subtle step-back motifs above the second-floor windows and the chevron-patterned lintels above the third-floor windows – contribute to the building's Zigzag styling.

LEFT The façade of the original three-storey brick building is symmetrical, and boasts a tall stone frontispiece. Fluted stone pilasters separate the window bays with their tan-coloured spandrel panels.

Westglen High School

10950 127th Street, Edmonton, Alberta

Rule, Wynn & Rule, 1940

Against a backdrop of Depression-era hardship, Edmonton taxpayers voted in three referendums against paying for a new high school in the city's west end. Controversy swirled whether monies collected from a from a four- to 16-percent cut in the salaries of teachers and administrators – which were intended for unemployment relief – actually went into the school board's building fund. In any event, the board spent $4,000 in April 1940 to acquire a 1.6-hectare plot. The new school was built in just six months.

The school's official opening ceremonies were attended by 1,500 residents, parents, and students, and featured presentations by the Glee Club, the Edmonton Schoolboys' Band, and individual students. The opening program noted that this "...beauteous streamlined edifice betokens the latest developments of education for this continent."

The school housed 12 classrooms, a science lab, spacious library, art room, staff rooms and a medical inspection room. It was anticipated that rooms, for homemaking and general shop instruction would be added at a later date. In the centre of the building was a combination auditorium / gymnasium that could accommodate championship basketball matches and seat 1,200 people for special events.

By 1957, the high school population had outgrown the facility, and it eventually became an elementary school.

LEFT The building's frontispiece features quarter-round edges, a horizontally proportioned window, raised period lettering, and symmetrical lamps that flank the front doors.

BOTTOM LEFT The two-storey, ivory stucco façade exemplifies Streamlined Moderne styling, from its flat roof, to the proportions of its horizontally banded windows, to the protruding speed-stripes decorating its walls. The trees obscuring the view were not present when the school was first built.

BOTTOM RIGHT The combination auditorium / gymnasium dominates this rear view of the school. Notice the streamlined protruding bands at its corners, plus the sloping external buttresses that help support the roof.

South Okanagan Secondary School

10332 – 350th Avenue, Oliver, British Columbia
Postle & Korner, 1945–48 (destroyed by fire, 2011)

After World War I, B.C. Premier 'Honest' John Oliver sought to create opportunities for returning veterans. He was responsible for the 1923 completion of a 40-kilometre concrete irrigation canal (known as 'the ditch') that transformed over 3,000 hectares of former desert into viable agricultural land. Besides producing tobacco and tomatoes, the village of Oliver – named after the premier – acquired the title of Cantaloupe Capital of Canada!

Following the Depression and World War II, there was a spirit of optimism and hope in the community that was expressed in the planning of the new school. Theodor Korner, the building's talented architect, sadly died of a heart attack in 1946 before seeing it completed.

The U-shaped structure's east wing housed academic classrooms while the west wing housed science and vocational rooms. The large gymnasium, basement cafeteria, and kitchen – plus the 700-seat auditorium at the bottom of the U – could be used when the school was closed. The building's sturdy concrete foundations equipped it to serve as a shelter in case of another war.

W.T. Straith, the provincial minister of education, officially opened the school on January 28, 1949, remarking: "You have the finest school in British Columbia... You should cherish it for it will remain the best for a long time." The opening's printed program boasted of the school's innovative materials, but local citizens thought the building was extravagant, nicknaming it the 'Taj Mahal.'

Tragically, while in the midst of a $29-million renovation, much of the original building caught fire in the early hours of September 12, 2011, destroying much of the structure. The remainder was demolished and a new, energy-efficient building was opened in February 2014.

TOP Seen here before its tragic destruction by fire in 2011, the auditorium at the south end of the school boasts such Streamlined Moderne features as the curved entrance block, horizontal banding at various points, and the large low-relief discs in the stucco at the upper level of the corners.

ABOVE This photo from a period postcard shows the two wings of the building; the auditorium is in the middle and the gymnasium at the extreme right.

Main Building, St. Louis College

165 Hébert Boulevard, Edmundston, New Brunswick
Edgar Courchesne, 1948

The area today known as Edmunston was once an important seasonal campground and meeting place for the Maliseet First Nation. The first Acadians arrived from St. Anne's Point (today's Fredericton), driven north by Loyalists fleeing America in the 1790s, while a steady influx of francophones from Quebec arrived in the 1800s. Originally named Petit-Sault (Little Falls) after the small rapids where the Madawaska flowed into the Saint John River, the settlement gained its present name in 1848, in honour of the colony of New Brunswick's then Lieutenant-Governor, Sir Edmund Walker Head.

Thanks to its extensive forests and location on the Saint John River, the village of Edmunston – population 1,800 – attracted its first sawmill in 1911; today, the paper industry is the city's largest industry.

A group of Eudist Fathers chose Edmundston in 1946 as the location for a boys' college offering a classical education; they named it St. Louis College after Monsigneur Louis Napoléon Dugal, a prominent religious teacher in the region. Classes in the early years were held in former military barracks. A provincial charter granted in 1947 gave the institution university status.

Quebec-born architect Edgar Courchesne, who had previously studied with Father Dom Bellot, drew up plans for a new building in 1948, which opened two years later. Like other contemporary Catholic structures in francophone New Brunswick, this building was more architecturally progressive than its English peers.

In 1980, the college's main building was named the Simon-Larouche Pavilion, to honour the college's first rector.

ABOVE This interior stair features stair treads with two-tone terrazzo, and a sleek rounded handrail detail.

LEFT The step-back detailing above the frontispiece's uppermost window resembles the smaller windows on the second level.

TOP A four-storey tower bearing a giant cross tops the building's five-storey, symmetrical main block, seen here in late afternoon sun. Clad in grey stone on the front facade, the middle floors feature rough stone pilasters separating smooth stretches of wall that are pierced by windows arranged in horizontal bands. Vertical strips of glass block illuminate the corner stair towers, which are topped by copper pavilion roofs.

Minto Memorial High School
126 Park Street, Minto, New Brunswick
Alward & Gillies, 1949

The official story is that the village of Minto – formerly known as Northfield – took its name in 1904 to mark the retirement of Gilbert John Elliot, the fourth Earl of Minto and Canada's eighth Governor General. Others believe, however, that the name arose two years earlier when some locals received a letter from Moncton bearing the name of that city's Minto Hotel, and adopted this name for their own use.

Nevertheless, Minto was the first recorded place in Canada from which coal was extracted and sold, being shipped to Boston as early as 1639, though coal mining only became widespread in the 1760s. Strip mining was employed because most of the coal was found only about eight metres below the surface.

The New Brunswick Central Railway line serving the coal industry reached Minto in 1904, and was extended to Fredericton nine years later.

Local coal was used to fuel the New Brunswick Power Corporation's nearby Grand Lake Generating Station, opened in 1931, but mining ceased around the time this station's operating licence expired in 2010.

Opened in 1949, Minto Memorial High School was one of the province's new schools that focused on improving sanitation and playground space. The architects employed a progressive style that avoided unnecessary architectural embellishment. Several additions have been made to the school since its opening.

ABOVE For added impact, the northwest-facing, curved stone front entrance with its three (formerly multiple-pane) windows is slightly recessed into the red brick wings. The vertical treatment of the two slightly protruding, two-storey exit door portals to the south contrast with the streamlined bands of intervening windows, which once had more distinctly horizontally proportioned panes.

Winnipeg Technical–Vocational High School

1555 Wall Street, Winnipeg, Manitoba

W.A. Martin, 1949–51

As Winnipeg was getting back on its feet after the Depression and World War II, it became clear that more than purely academic schooling was required to serve the needs of the city's expanding population and to address technological advancements in the workplace. Parents welcomed the incorporation of sports, music festivals, and hobby clubs into school programs, all of which helped keep students in the classroom longer and out of trouble.

An early school to adopt a broader curriculum was Winnipeg Technical–Vocational High School, widely known as Tec-Voc. Located in the city's east end, it offered classes in subjects ranging from hairdressing to aerospace to culinary arts. Its renowned music program mounted annual Gilbert and Sullivan operettas and later musicals, plus folk-song choirs in the early years, as well as the ever-popular Tec-Voc Marching Band. Sports teams ('Home of the Hornets') achieved enviable results across a range of disciplines.

Designed by the school board's building commissioner, the building is a superb example of Art Deco, echoing the optimism and forward thinking of the age. It is considered the crowning achievement of architect W.A. Martin's 30-year career.

The school underwent several additions in the 1960s, and today is home to over 1,300 students.

LEFT This semi-circular northern entrance echoes the curved corners found on the front façade. The slogan 'Knowledge without practice makes but half an artist' is engraved in the limestone panel above the doors.

ABOVE The sidewalls of the main entrance staircase echo the façade's bold curves. Notice the 'rule of three' grooves in the stone, a telltale characteristic of Streamlined Moderne decoration.

TOP Taller than the rest of the school, the main entrance block in the east-facing entrance façade features uninterrupted stone pilasters with subtle Zigzag detailing that contrast with the Streamlined corner treatment of the spaces on either side. Three floors of windows with horizontally proportioned panes, interspersed with sections of limestone, are separated by bands of red brick. The provincial coat of arms is one of the carved emblems at the roofline.

Hospitals

Saint John General Hospital

Waterloo Street at Alma Street, Saint John, New Brunswick

Pond, Pond, Martin & Lloyd; Alward & Gillies (associates), 1930–31 (demolished 1995)

Opened in 1865, Saint John's 150-bed General Public Hospital was deemed in the late 1920s to be insufficient to meet the needs of this port city. Rather than attempting to upgrade it, the hospital's Board of Commissioners elected to build a new structure.

The Chicago architectural firm of Pond, Pond, Martin & Lloyd was hired for the project, with Irving Pond taking the lead in the hospital's design. The construction contract for the 300-bed facility was valued at $1.16 million; the city's warden laid its cornerstone on August 3, 1930.

The buff-brick and cut-stone structure, built on a reinforced-concrete frame, dominated the city's skyline. Its plan consisted of three radiating wings plus a small courtyard to the rear. Floors three through six housed wards of four to six beds each; the sixth floor nursery had cots for 32 infants; the seventh was the surgical ward, while the eighth floor was for children. The ninth floor contained a solarium with views in three directions.

After it had been closed for about 10 years, the building was demolished in a dramatic contained explosion in 1995. The hospital's dome survived the demolition, and now shelters a gazebo in a city park. A parking lot today occupies some of the site of this once-grand structure.

TOP This archival photo of the south-facing façade was taken just before the hospital's opening in 1931. While the 11-storey dome, step-back massing, and the stone piers above the front entry lent a sense of Zigzag verticality, the stone banding stretching across the upper floors tied the composition together. The rounded-arch entry doors and upper windows confirm that the architects had not fully abandoned more traditional forms.

LEFT Subtle details on the façade are evident in this 1994 photo, taken a year prior to demolition. Notice the streamlined stone and brick bands on the upper floors, and the series of vertical zigzags in the 45-degree corner of the main tower.

Library and Archives Canada, Alward & Gillies Collection, 1988-122 2000753319 and 1979-122 2000753319

ABOVE The period decorative elements of the luxurious front lobby included the bas-relief motifs atop the fluted pilasters framing the stairs and the fireplace, and the geometric treatment of metal railings and the chandeliers.

Verdun General Hospital

400 Lasalle Boulevard, Montreal, Quebec

Alphonse Venne, 1930–31

The roots of today's community of Verdun, situated on the southwest shore of the island of Montreal, date back to the time of the fur trade. A French settler, Zacharie Dupuis – the leader of a militia against the Iroquois to protect this valuable portage route – was granted a 130-hectare plot of land in return for his service. Shortly after, the stronghold gained the name Verdun, in honour of Dupuis's hometown of Saverdun in the south of France.

In the early 1900s, the town grew as Montreal gained more industry, becoming a city in 1912. The arrival of a tram linking it to downtown, and the construction of flood protection, dramatically boosted the city's population to 60,000 residents by 1931. Although the city resisted annexation by annexation by the City of Montreal in the 1930s, it was one of the 27 smaller municipalities that was merged with Montreal as part of that city's amalgamation in 2002.

Arsène Joseph-Richard, a Canadian Catholic priest and president of the local school board, worked in 1928 to found Verdun General Hospital to serve the fast-growing city, dedicating it to Christ the King. Constructed in 1930–31, the hospital opened on May 1, 1932. A wing was added to the building in 1944; today, it is affiliated with the faculty of medicine at the University of Montreal, and employs nearly 1,600 people.

MIDDLE The highlight of the five-storey symmetrical hospital is the tall central entrance block that's capped with a copper-covered pyramidal roof bearing an illuminated cross. Protruding, flat-roof rectangular blocks with half-octagonal balconies define the corners of the central tower and the two ends of the façade.

TOP The hospital is a fine example of the Zigzag style, thanks to its step-back massing and multiple plans. Simplified floral detailing embellishes various parts of its façade, including the large yellowish terra-cotta panels directly beneath the tower roof, the carved stone vertical panels above the windows, and the matching motif in the metal balcony railings. Slightly protruding, two-storey exit door portals to the south contrast with the streamlined bands of intervening windows, which once had more distinctly horizontally proportioned panes.

BOTTOM A continuous band of triangles and chevrons – pure Zigzag-style decoration – separate the top of the ground-level stone from the brick wall above.

Administration Building, Vancouver General Hospital

715 West Twelfth Avenue, Vancouver, British Columbia

Townley & Matheson, 1943

The founding of Vancouver General Hospital dates back to 1886, when a tent was erected to treat workers involved in building the final stretch of the Canadian Pacific Railway. After the tent succumbed to fire that June, it was replaced by a one-storey building with nine beds.

In 1906, hospital operations moved to a new, three-storey stone building on Fairview ridge, overlooking False Creek. The building, later known as the Heather Pavilion, was quickly expanded to the north. Additional facilities were required to meet the growing need for healthcare, and the University of British Columbia's move to its present-day Point Grey campus made space available for new construction. The hospital's infectious disease building was opened in 1926, and a tuberculosis facility in 1936.

When King George VI and Queen Elizabeth drove past the hospital on May 29 during the 1939 Royal Visit to Canada, ambulatory patients, as well as those confined to gurneys, lined Twelfth Avenue to catch a glimpse of the royal couple in their open car, which was prohibited from driving faster than 30 kilometres per hour.

November 1, 1943 marked the opening of a new, four-storey, Streamlined Moderne building – designed by the hospital's preferred architectural firm of Townley & Matheson – that housed administrative offices, the semi-private ward, physiotherapy and laboratory facilities, as well as a new outpatient department. Although it presently serves as a health centre, the building's days are numbered; it and a nearby structure are slated to be demolished and replaced by an eight-storey modern facility devoted to the treatment of mental health and addictions.

TOP This H-shaped hospital administration building is a stellar example of Streamlined Moderne design. Dominating the façade are horizontal bands that contain metal-frame windows and boast incised speed stripes that wrap around the building corners. Notice the bullnose treatment of the wall framing the vertical bands of glass block in the end walls.

RIGHT The solid concrete sidewalls of the front steps feature a bullnose front and incised speed stripes. Above the main entrance, rounded half-columns with vertically ribbed spandrels lend a vertical emphasis to the central portion of the façade.

St. Joseph's Auxiliary Hospital

10722 – 82nd (Whyte) Avenue, Edmonton, Alberta

George Heath MacDonald, 1945 & 1955

Founded in 1861 in Kingston, Ontario, the Sisters of Providence of St. Vincent de Paul is a group of Catholic women that to this day provides compassionate and loving care to the poor and oppressed. For many years, the Sisters ministered by building schools and hospitals, but now are engaged in advocacy on a range of social issues.

The Sisters' efforts in Edmonton began in 1915 when they assumed responsibility for a hostel for immigrant women and girls; in 1923 they opened an orphanage serving 56 boys aged three to 16. Edmonton's Archbishop O'Leary asked the Sisters in 1927 to transform a 1912 apartment building – in a neighbourhood known today as Garneau – into the city's first home for the elderly. Three years later, the facility was converted to an official hospital known as St. Joseph's Hospital for the Chronically Ill.

Design began in 1945 on a new four-storey building that would house 150 beds. The $400,000 structure was officially opened on January 24, 1948; later that year it led the way in providing care during Edmonton's Poliomyelitis outbreak, which claimed the lives of six of the 88 people afflicted. Two more floors, which were anticipated in the additional plan, were added in 1955 to provide chronic care beds. A decade later, projecting wings were added at either end for a convent residence and chapel. The building continued to provide extended care services as an auxiliary hospital until it was closed in 1993.

The building took on a new life when it was respectfully converted in 1997 to a condominium complex known, not surprisingly, as The Garneau.

TOP The frontispiece displays the building's combination of Zigzag and Streamlined Moderne styling. The vertical treatment of the central windows and stone spandrels, some with incised chevrons, are offset by the wraparound corner windows. Before becoming a condo, the inscription above the doors read 'St. Joseph's Hospital,' and the pointed arch niches flanking the doors contained religious statues. The metalwork on the front doors is a sympathetic modern interpretation of the building's decoration.

RIGHT The addition of balconies and a seventh floor, as part of the 1990s conversion to a condominium, has partially obscured but not eliminated the original hospital's Art Deco features. It is believed that the original four-storey design did not include any glass block or horizontal stone speed stripes. The Gothic-style windows at the east end mark the location of the former chapel. Notice how the building's red brick and limestone are carried through into the modern additions to the right.

Winnipeg Public Baths

381 Sherbrook Street, Winnipeg, Manitoba

Pratt & Ross, 1930–31

The construction of a new public bath (swimming pool) in Winnipeg was authorized by city council in 1929, after the sudden discovery of structural weakness in its 1915 predecessor. The initial allocation of $150,000 for its construction had to be increased by $10,000 to complete the land acquisition and allow more of the submitted tenders to qualify. As a Depression relief project with significant federal funding at stake, there was urgency to get the work underway. Architect Ralph Benjamin Pratt took the lead role in the building's design.

The opening ceremony for the pool took place on the last day of February 1931, and featured demonstrations of diving, lifesaving, swimming, and a performance by 'Mrs. Harrison's Waterbabies' – a troop of teenage girls led by the wife of the superintendent of public baths.

The reinforced concrete structure with a steel beam roof was the first Olympic-sized pool in Winnipeg. In its first year, it played host to a much-publicized 'Manitoba vs. U.S.A.' swimming showdown; sadly, Seattle's Helene Madison out-swam Manitoban aquatic star Vera Tustin. Sherbrook was also the city's first pool, in 1946, to offer Red Cross instruction.

In the late 1980s, the need for repairs arose; the Friends of Sherbook Pool was established in 1992 to battle the threats of closing the building. After a series of crises, the pool now has a new roof and bleachers, thanks to $4.2 million in funding from the city, province, and the Kinsmen Club of Winnipeg. The pool reopened in February 2017.

TOP Zigzag principles are evident at the front entrance, including the multiple-plane treatment at the building corners and the step-back motif on the limestone caps atop the pilasters. Regrettably, the windows on the main façade were lowered from their original placement, compromising the sense of balance.

LEFT In keeping with the Zigzag style, protruding Alsip red brick pilasters separate the vertical windows that are arranged in groups of three.

Women's Tribute Memorial Lodge

200 Woodlawn Street, Winnipeg, Manitoba
Northwood & Chivers, 1930–31

The story of this structure began on April 24, 1917, when a group of influential Winnipeg women began raising money for the creation of a permanent memorial honouring Manitoba's heroes from the World War I. Their Foundation Tribute Night the next month raised over $16,500 in cash and pledges; an amount that, when matched with a $9,000 contribution from the Deer Lodge branch of the Canadian Legion in 1930, enabled the project to proceed.

Manitoba architects George W. Northwood and Cyril W.U. Chivers, both veterans of World War I, were commissioned to design the building, which opened in the fall of 1931. More than just a monument, it contained an auditorium, billiards room, clubrooms, and a kitchen to help veterans carry on their lives as civilians, plus a Room of Silence to help them remember all those who had served their province and country.

The design was noteworthy for including one of the first wheelchair accessibility ramps, for "ex-service men who might find it convenient to make use of."

With a recent addition to its north side, the building now houses a movement disorders clinic; it is owned by the Winnipeg Regional Health Authority.

LEFT Boldly geometric, frosted-glass ceiling fixtures from the original building still illuminate parts of the interior.

TOP The top portion of the main façade features a low-relief carving of Manitoba's provincial emblem – the St. George's cross above a bison. Its Zigzag elements include the multiple planes found in the brickwork piers, the step-back parapet, and the period lettering.

ABOVE The two-storey building is constructed of buff brick with Tyndall limestone trim. Its purpose was to "serve as a tribute to the veterans of the Great War who have returned, and a memorial to those who have not returned."

Hogan Bath

2188 Wellington Street, Montreal, Quebec

David Jerome Spence, 1931–32

According to some sources, three-quarters of the homes in rapidly expanding working-class districts in Montreal in 1905 included only a sink and a toilet, with no hot water and no bath.

Initially, for reasons of public hygiene – and later, as a works program during the Depression – the City of Montreal constructed public bath buildings in various neighbourhoods to serve the residents of these 'cold-water flats.' At its peak, the city operated a total of 18 such facilities, the most of any city in North America. These public baths typically included a swimming pool, lavatories, and showers with hot water. They were open year-round and admission was free.

The Hogan Bath, across the street from Marguerite Bourgeoys Park in the city's Pointe-Saint-Charles neighbourhood, was named after the neighbourhood alderman, Francis J. Hogan, who served from 1924 to 1927.

In the 1940s, as living standards improved and full bathrooms in homes became more popular, public baths like the Hogan took on new roles as community swimming pools. A December 1944 article in the *Montreal Gazette* describes a swim meet involving school children from across the island, held at the Hogan, that also featured a swimming demonstration by Dominion champion Jean Marc Demers.

Closed in 1995 and later sold to a developer, the Hogan Bath was transformed into a 17-unit condominium named the Hogan Lofts.

ABOVE The symmetrical main block of the Hogan Bath is sheathed in smooth artificial stone blocks, while the wing that contained the swimming pool (visible to the right) is clad in red brick. The frontispiece of the Zigzag façade boasts step-back massing, multiple planes, and a variety of vertical grooves, making it seem taller than its two-storey height. Notice the French and English words for 'bath' that appear at either side of the façade, protruding from an accordion-style horizontal stone band that terminates with a pair of speed stripes. Originally, chandeliers flanked the front entrance, and industrial-style windows contained smaller panes of glass.

Club Building, Fraternal Order of Eagles

135 Bastion Street, Nanaimo, British Columbia

McCarter & Nairne, 1934

The roots of the Fraternal Order of Eagles date back to 1898, when six of Seattle's competing theatre owners were facing a musician's strike. Once they'd agreed how to deal with the strike, they chose to band together in a benevolent organization they called the Order of Good Things. Membership grew as touring playwrights, actors, and stagehands met on local theatre stages, then went on to share the Order's story across North America. Nanaimo's branch was formed in 1899.

In 1927, the membership renamed the organization the Fraternal Order of Eagles, adopted the bald eagle as their symbol, and created the Auxiliary for women. The lodges where Eagles held their meetings were known as aeries, named after the lofty nests where eagles dwell.

Eagles members were pioneers in fulfilling their motto of 'People Helping People.' They founded Mother's Day back in 1904; U.S. Eagles were a driving force behind the Social Security Act that was introduced in 1935 by American president Franklin D. Roosevelt, himself a life-long Eagle.

Though they may seem antiquated by today's standards, fraternal orders played an important part in urban life. Before the advent of universal healthcare and government pensions, they provided such benefits to their members – especially important in a coal-mining community like Nanaimo, where workplace accidents were very frequent. The Fraternal Order of Eagles is still active, with 4,000 members in British Columbia and 800,000 across North America.

Nanaimo's Eagles' hall – designed by the prominent Vancouver architectural firm of McCarter & Nairne – contained all the amenities needed for the club life. Behind the four storefronts facing Bastion Street lay a men's lounge and cloakroom, a smaller ladies' lounge and powder room, and the secretary's office. Running the full width of the second floor was the lodge room, behind which was the assembly hall, cloakroom, and kitchen with adjoining women's lavatory. The basement housed three cards rooms, a recreation room with a fireplace and bar, a billiards room, and a space for carpet bowling.

After the Eagles vacated the building, the upper floor became home to dance studios; its Art Deco light fixtures, main staircase, and dance halls with their sprung wooden floors all remained intact. Over the past several years, the building's owners have partially restored the exterior to its former glory.

ABOVE The roofline is adorned with multi-layer concrete chevrons, while a bold geometric shape – perhaps representing an eagle in flight – tops the second-floor windows.

TOP RIGHT Created in cast concrete, a giant bas-relief eagle on a step-back perch guards the front entrance to the club. Notice the chevron patterns beneath its wings, and the subtle speed-stripes atop the bullnose walls framing the windows that flank the front door.

BOTTOM RIGHT Constructed of reinforced concrete with a wooden truss roof, the two-storey building's façade incorporates such Zigzag features as bas-relief chevrons and bevelled corner pilasters.

Domaine d'Esterel

Ste-Marguerite-du-Lac-Masson, Quebec
Antoine Courtens, 1936–38

After quarreling with his brother over the management of the enormous fortune bequeathed to them by their deceased father – the Belgian industrialist Baron Édouard Empain – Louis Empain set his sights on promoting Belgian affairs in Canada. Having fallen in love with the Laurentians region of Quebec, he purchased 7,000 hectares of land in the summer of 1935, mostly on a peninsula on Lac Masson, just east of Ste-Agathe-des-Monts.

Empain's vision was to establish what we would describe today as a four-season luxury resort complex catering to wealthy Europeans living in North America. Arriving by plane, train, or automobile, guests could swim, ride horses, play tennis, hunt, fish, skate, or ski. Empain named the complex Domaine d'Esterel, after the Mediterranean coastal mountain range in southeastern France, and hired Belgian architect Antoine Courtens, well-versed in European Modernism, to bring his plan to life.

Accommodation options included the hilltop hotel, modern villas, and log cabins dotting the lakeshore. The complex also included a commercial building, an indoor sports facility, tennis courts, a lakeside sports club, riding stables, ski lodge, and even a hydroplane landing facility!

Work began in September 1936, with the Hôtel de la Pointe-Bleue receiving its first guests in May 1937. The following February, the commercial building opened; it housed luxury shops (including a Holt Renfrew boutique), a cinema, exhibition hall, plus the famed Blue Room restaurant-cabaret. The architectural styling was unlike that of any other resort complex in eastern North America.

The good times ended abruptly with the declaration of war in September 1939. Acting on rumours that Empain was a German spy, the Canadian government seized Domaine d'Esterel and used it to train Canadian soldiers. Shocked by this occupation, Empain decided to sell the complex after the war; the sale was finally completed in 1957.

In the 1970s, the hotel became a nursing home, and the commercial building served as administrative space for the municipality of Ste-Marguerite. While the hotel was tragically demolished several years ago, the commercial building was finally designated as a provincial historical site in 2014.

ABOVE Seen here in a vintage photo, the three-storey commercial building overlooking Lac Masson featured a bold streamlined façade. The reinforced concrete frame was clad in wood and finished with white-painted stucco. At the front is a small gas station.

Domaine d'Esterel

ABOVE Located on the second floor of the commercial building, the sleek Blue Room restaurant-cabaret opened on July 9, 1937. Guests danced to the music of Benny Goodman's jazz orchestra.

TOP RIGHT The recently demolished *Hôtel de la Pointe-Bleu* was located on a hilltop near the tip of the peninsula. Notice its horizontal bands of windows, offset by the semicircular glazed stairwell cylinder.

MIDDLE RIGHT The lakeside 'Sporting Club,' since demolished, featured simple rectilinear and curved blocks with horizontal and vertical windows.

BOTTOM RIGHT As seen in this 2005 photo, the staircase from the ground floor to the second floor of the commercial building is a study in streamlined design. The vertical band of square windows in the taller south-facing portion provides a strong counterpoint to the large east-facing curved wall.

Royal Canadian Legion Memorial Hall

1820 Cornwall Street, Regina, Saskatchewan

Storey & Van Egmond, 1947–51

The origins of the Royal Canadian Legion – known to many of us as the organization from which we buy poppies for Remembrance Day – date back to World War I. The Great War Veterans Association, established in 1917, joined with similar groups in 1926 to become the Canadian Legion of the British Empire Service League that had been founded in 1921 by Field Marshals Earl Haig and Jan Smuts.

In the years following, the Legion expanded quickly, focused on helping veterans get re-established back in Canada by offering advice on government pensions and other benefits. The institution became the Royal Canadian Legion in 1960.

The Regina branch is known as Branch No. 1 since it was the first to receive its charter, in 1926. The design of the present Legion building began in the summer of 1945; Princess Elizabeth and the Duke of Edinburgh presided at the official opening of the $335,000 building on October 17, 1951. At its peak, Branch No. 1 had some 2,500 members.

Like other Legions across the country, the Regina branch's membership declined significantly over time. To deal with the financial challenge, Branch No. 1 took the radical step in 2013 of demolishing the rear of its building – containing the Atlantic Auditorium, Lancaster Lounge, and Dieppe Cafeteria – to make way for a parkade. Untouched are the Memorial Hall and the Peace Tower, which feature stained-glass windows and five murals, painted by K.C. Lockhead, that celebrate the province's military history.

LEFT While the fluted corner pilasters with floral capitals lend Stripped Classical formality, the band of chevrons and sunbursts above the large window add some Zigzag flair. The small carved panels high up on the recessed second-floor wall depict a bison and a wheat sheaf (left), and a lion with three sheaves of wheat. The vividly coloured stained-glass window, entitled Saskatchewan for Freedom, features a sailor, aviator, soldier, and nurse, and is accompanied by the biblical inscription, 'They shall beat their swords into plow shares.'

BOTTOM LEFT The façade of the two-storey Legion, shown here before the demolition of its rear portion, is built of light brown brick with Tyndall limestone trim. The verticality of the entrance block offsets the horizontal stone banding at the roofline and above the windows.

Total Abstinence Society Building

342 Duckworth Street, St. John's, Newfoundland

William J. Ryan, late 1940s

Irish-born Roman Catholic priest Kyran Walsh was responsible for introducing St. John's to the temperance movement back in 1841. In 1850, members of the Newfoundland Total Abstinence Society were given a medal bearing the words 'Be Sober and Watch' and took the famous pledge: "I pledge myself with the Divine Assistance that as long as I shall continue a member of this Society I will abstain from all intoxicating liquors unless for medical or religious purposes and that I will discountenance intemperance in others."

By the end of the nineteenth century, the renamed Total Abstinence and Benefit Society attracted a sizeable membership, growing to become one of the city's leading fraternal organizations. Its band played at civic functions, while members of its Cricket and Boating Club took part in the annual St. John's Regatta.

In the late 1940s, the Society hired local architect William J. Ryan to design for it a speculative office building, located on Duckworth Street, just a few blocks up the hill from the harbour.

An early occupant of the structure was CBC Radio St. John's, which also used some adjoining space from the then-empty Capitol Theatre. CBC delivered its last broadcast from the building on April 27, 2007; the Society had previously ceased operations in 1985. The building lay vacant for five years, before a developer began renovations; the plans call for the addition of several floors in order to reopen the structure as the Marconi condominium building.

LEFT This double-height glass-block window is recessed into the facade of the three-storey side wing. To the left, the Streamlined horizontal bands that wrap around the corner are interspersed with solid panels bearing semicircular vertical fluting.

TOP The front façade of the six-storey, cast-in-place concrete structure – seen here in 1994 while the CBC still occupied the building – boasts a careful balance of vertical and horizontal elements. Its original colour scheme featured a mix of gray and off-white tones, with alternating bands of dark red. Notice the Zigzag-style multiple planes and step-back massing of the slender frontispiece, and the band of decorative circles-within-squares embellishing the parapet.

Victoria Park Filtration Plant

2701 Queen Street East, Toronto, Ontario
Thomas Pomphrey, 1928–41

Outbreaks of typhoid fever and the ensuing political scandals led to the resignation in 1912 of the City of Toronto's Works Commissioner Charles Rust. Replacing him was an up-and-coming fellow named Roland Caldwell Harris, whose first job with the city was as an office boy at the age of 12.

Upon becoming Works Commissioner, Harris cast aside a newly completed city report on the future of the Toronto's water supply, and commissioned his own. Harris's report advocated locating a much-needed new water intake and filtration system on the sloping site of Victoria Park, just past the city's eastern boundary, as well as adding a reservoir and pumping station at another location.

Little happened to his 1913 plan because of World War I and resistance from city council, but in 1923 the Victoria Park land was finally expropriated. The 1926 'Report on Proposed Extensions to the Water Works System' by consulting engineers H.G. Acres and William Gore echoed the 1913 plan; the next year, city council approved the entire Water Works Extension Project.

In 1928, William Storrie of the engineering firm Gore, Naismith & Storrie submitted preliminary drawings for the Filtration Plant, but Harris found them 'plain and unattractive.' In response, the firm put their in-house architect, Thomas Canfield Pomphrey, on the project. Some 17 months later, the plant's design had been essentially finalized.

Although much of the construction was completed by 1932, the first purified water was not pumped until November 1, 1941. The complex was officially renamed the R.C. Harris Water Treatment Plant in 1945 upon Harris's death.

The plant gained the nickname 'The Palace of Purification' after playing an important role in Michael Ondaatje's novel *In the Skin of a Lion*; beyond standing in for a prison, asylum, and corporate headquarters in numerous movies and TV series, it was featured in the 1983 Canadian comedy film *Strange Brew*, which starred the legendary 'hoser' characters Bob & Doug McKenzie of *SCTV* fame.

The complex consisted of a carefully arranged set of building masses, each performing a distinct function. Closest to the lake was the Pump House, which took in lake water and propelled it to the nearby Service Building, where alum was added as the first step of purification. The water then travelled uphill to

underground mixing chambers and settling ponds, before it flowed into the twin filtering pools in the western wing of the Filtration Building. Finally, after being chlorinated, water entered storage reservoirs before ultimately flowing into the city's water supply network.

In 1957, the planned eastern wing of the Filtration Building was completed, nearly doubling the plant's capacity. The facility was named a National Historic Civil Engineering Site in 1992, and designated under the Ontario Heritage Act in 1998. As the city's largest water treatment plant, the facility today supplies up to 47 percent of the water for the City of Toronto and York Region.

ABOVE The various buildings comprising the plant are seen in this July 2016 aerial view (shot while some construction work was taking place). Closest to Lake Ontario is the Pump House; immediately behind it is the Service Building with the Alum Tower. Up the hill is the Terrace, and centred behind it, the Administration Building. Extending from its sides are the eastern and western wings of the Filtration Building, each more than 100 metres in length. A paved roadway with a hairpin turn links the various buildings.

Victoria Park Filtration Plant

TOP LEFT Terrazzo floors with marble inlays, polished brass control panels, and an enormous skylight supported by rounded arches make the Filtration Building a truly distinctive interior space.

BOTTOM RIGHT This sensational bas-relief carving depicting a turbine between matching spirals of flowing water is found atop all four sides of the Pump House.

ABOVE On the western wing (and the matching eastern wing) of the Filtration Building, protruding brick and stone pilasters, topped by pointed stone merlons, divide the long façade into bays corresponding to the filtering pools within. The round-arch windows that illuminate the filtering pools match the shape of the upper-floor windows in the Administration Building.

TOP RIGHT Like the rest of the complex, the Pump House was built of light yellow-grey buff brick with Queenston limestone trim. This view of its southeast corner reveals many of the plant's Stripped Classical attributes, including smooth stone pilasters and dentils, plus diagonal courses of protruding brick. The detailing of the stone trim flanking the arched windows – halves of pointed stone merlons with multiple-plane discs below – matches the treatment of the Filtration Building's pilasters.

ABOVE LEFT At the intersection of the two wings of the Filtration Building is the marble-and-bronze control pylon, which displays information about the filtration process. Notice the bold, multi-coloured pattern in the floor, pointing to the different components of the plant.

TOP RIGHT Directly in front of the Administration Building is the Terrace, whose front face includes an arched niche containing a bronze fountain. The keystone atop the terrace niche, and the main entrance behind, is carved to represent rushing water.

ABOVE This stone detail, appearing at the top level of the central block of the Administration Building, features a roundel of the Toronto Water Works (TWW) monogram framed by folded scallop shells.

Administration Building, Glenmore Water Treatment Plant

1668 – 56 Avenue Southwest, Calgary, Alberta

Thomas Pomphrey, 1929–34

The Glenmore neighbourhood in the southwestern section of today's City of Calgary acquired its name in the 1860s, when a settler named Sam Livingston built a home in the valley of the Elbow River, and named the valley Glenmore (Gaelic for 'big valley') after his hometown in County Kilkenny, Ireland.

The natural flow of the Elbow River was interrupted by the completion of the giant Glenmore dam on January 31, 1933, which soon held back 16 billion litres of water. The resulting Glenmore Reservoir, four square kilometres in area, today provides southern Calgary with its drinking water – and a place for citizens to sail, row, and paddle canoes, as well as fish for perch, pike, whitefish, and trout.

In order to be fit for drinking, the reservoir's water – periodically laden with silt – needed to be purified. The Glenmore Water Treatment Plant was planned by engineering firm Gore, Nasmith & Storrie, with architectural design by their in-house architect Thomas Pomphrey, who was concurrently working on the Victoria Park Filtration Plant in Toronto.

The Glenmore plant consisted of the Administration Building, an attached Filtration Building (where the water was treated), and the Alum Tower (that stored minerals used in purification). On account of its location close to the city, surrounded by parkland, the building was deemed an important civic structure warranting an architect's attention.

With the inclusion of the pumping station and pipeline, the entire Glenmore Water Works System project cost over $4 million, making it one of the most noteworthy feats of engineering in Western Canada. When it opened, the plant could purify 105 million litres per day, well in excess of the needs of Calgary's 200,000 residents at the time. With construction occurring at the start of the Depression, the plant was considered a make-work project, employing local businesses and numerous workers.

When massive flooding struck Calgary in June 2013, the plant's purification was not interrrupted, even though river water spilled over the dam.

The architectural style of the Administration Building's exterior is Stripped Classical; its elegant interior – whose second-floor offices are reached by a grand staircase – boasts travertine limestone floors, marble walls, and a plaster ceiling with decorative cornice moldings. By contrast, the Filtration Building has terrazzo floors and green tiled walls, and is illuminated by clerestory windows.

TOP The Stripped Classical façade of the three-storey, hipped-roof Administration Building consists of unadorned Tyndall limestone pilasters framing stretches of pressed red brick. The second level features multiple-pane metal-sash windows, while nautical-themed porthole windows decorate the upper portion. The slightly protruding doorframe of the stone vestibule is capped by a carved wave motif, upon which sits a 'CWW' (Calgary Water Works) hexagonal emblem.

RIGHT The Alum tower, to the rear of the Administration Building, exhibits subtle multiple-plane treatment in the brickwork with only modest stone trim.

Seven Sisters Generating Station

On the Winnipeg River near Whitemouth, Manitoba

F.H. Martin (consulting engineer), 1929–31 & 1948–52

Back in the 1730s, French-Canadian explorer Sieur Pierre de la Vérendrye came upon an 11-kilometre stretch of the Winnipeg River that contained seven rapids. It was the water tumbling over these rapids that was to be harnessed two centuries later at the Seven Sisters Generating Station.

During the 1880s and 1890s, enterprises such as the Manitoba Electric & Gas Light Company competed with one another to power electric street railways and illuminate streets and businesses. (Only a few homes had electric lights; the rest relied on kerosene lamps.) Over the following decades, a number of companies arose to develop, transmit, and distribute electricity in the province.

The first hydroelectric generating station, serving the City of Brandon, opened in 1900 but operated for less than a year. Six years later, the first year-round dam at Pinawa opened on a branch of the Winnipeg River, followed by several other dams over the next two decades. In the 1920s, several dozen smaller communities were connected to the Manitoba Power Company's grid, increasing the demand for electricity.

In July 1929, the Winnipeg Electric Company began construction of the powerhouse for the Seven Sisters Generating Station, completing it just over two years later. Three of its eventual six turbines tapped the 18.6-metre drop in water level, producing 75 megawatts of power.

The second stage of the station was begun in 1948 and finally completed in 1952, doubling the electrical output. Today, Seven Sisters' seven transmission lines carry its power primarily to Winnipeg, but also eastward to Kenora.

BOTTOM LEFT The giant concrete mass of the powerhouse contains subtle traces of Art Deco styling. Notice the recessed speed stripes that wrap around the top, offsetting the numerous vertical windows.

LEFT Splendid wave motifs adorn the tops of the tall, multi-pane windows that bring daylight into the station's turbine hall. Notice the multiple-plane detailing that flanks the windows, accentuating the structure's height.

McPhillips Street Pumping Station

360 McPhillips Street, Winnipeg, Manitoba
William Fingland, 1930

Prior to the turn of the twentieth century, Winnipeg's water was supplied by 'watermen' who led oxcarts carrying barrels of untreated water that was drawn from the Red and Assiniboine Rivers. When this sewage-laden water was deemed undrinkable, the city resorted to digging several large artesian wells, but their hard water could also be perilously unhealthy. Canada's third-largest city – which dreamed of being the 'Chicago of the North' – was badly served by its discoloured water that smelled and tasted foul. In 1905 alone, 1,600 citizens became ill from typhoid fever, while another 133 souls perished.

The visionary but costly remedy – overwhelmingly agreed-to by Winnipeggers in a 1913 public vote – involved bringing water by aqueduct from pristine Shoal Lake, which straddled the Manitoba–Ontario border some 140 kilometres away, and sat nearly 90 metres in elevation higher than the city.

A special railway was required to build the enclosed concrete aqueduct, but on April 6, 1919, the first water from Shoal Lake flowed into the city's reservoirs. The grand project, costing $17 million to complete, has supplied water to Winnipeg ever since.

Meanwhile, the city had opened a water pumping station and reservoir on McPhillips Street in 1907, yet less than two decades later, despite opposition from local residents, city council voted to build a new, larger pumping station and reservoir adjacent to the older facility. It began operating in 1930; during a 1933 tour, the *Winnipeg Tribune*'s city editor noted that "off the tiled floor you could eat the proverbial meal."

Time marched on, and the 1930 pumping station also proved to be undersized. Although a new station and covered reservoir opened in 1968, this Art Deco structure lives on as a city maintenance and storage garage.

TOP This 1992 photo reveals the simplicity of the symmetrical façade of the all-concrete building. Single smaller piers separate each window, while wider and taller piers topped by a subtle vertical groove separate each group of three windows.

RIGHT The multiple planes and step-back massing of the bevel-topped corner piers lends a Zigzag touch to the frontispiece. The distinctive pattern of the glass blocks in the vertical windows involves larger square blocks flanking a stacked pair of half-sized blocks.

LIFE AT
HOME

This chapter introduces dwellings constructed in the Art Deco style. It profiles apartment buildings situated on busy thoroughfares and quiet neighbourhood streets, plus grand and more modest single-family residences located in larger cities and small towns.

The Glen Grove

2837 Yonge Street, Toronto, Ontario
Kaplan & Sprachman, 1930–31

Part of the reason Toronto expanded northward in the final decades of the 1800s was the extension of its street car network. The Metropolitan Street Railway, operating horse-drawn street cars on a single track on the west side of Yonge Street, reached Glengrove Avenue in 1886; the railway was electrified five years later. The neighbourhood of North Toronto was incorporated as a town in 1890, and annexed by the City of Toronto in 1912. Nine years later, Toronto's streetcar system was taken over by the newly formed Toronto Transit Commission, with night service being added on the Yonge line in July 1932. The presence of this transit service undoubtedly influenced the decision to locate the Glen Grove Apartments at the northeast corner of Yonge Street and Glengrove Avenue, overlooking the Lawrence Park ravine.

The building housed 68 suites; a period trade journal noted that the "equipment in the apartments is of the highest order, including electric range, electric refrigerators and built-in kitchen cabinets." The article also pointed out that each suite was equipped with a wall safe to protect the occupant's valuables. Garage space was provided at the rear of the building, but the city's building code at the time prohibited a direct connection from the garage to the building.

The Glen Grove is noteworthy as being one of Canada's few apartment buildings with Zigzag-style decoration, although its façade possesses various streamlined features. Its architects, Kaplan & Sprachman, designed many private homes and apartments, but would go on to become Canada's most prolific designers of movie theatres across the country, a number of which are profiled later in the book.

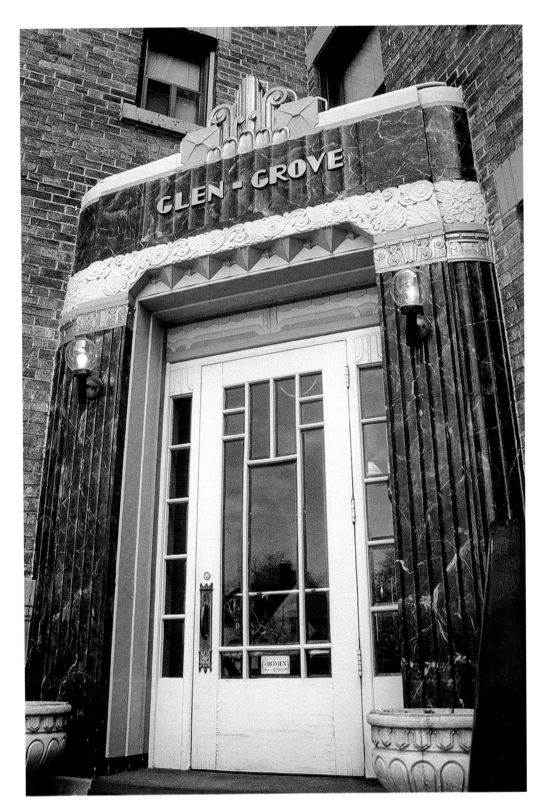

RIGHT The front entrance – with its multiple planes, period lettering and crowning floral motif – is a fine example of Zigzag design. Notice the stylish geometry of the glass panes in the front door. Originally, the entrance was exposed stone; seen here in 1993, a faux-marble and gilded finish has been added. Presently, it is painted solid black.

The Glen Grove

ABOVE The original metal grilles that embellished the façade in selected locations are still present, as seen in this contemporary photo. The stone lintels are decorated with subtle floral details flanked by vertical grooves.

TOP RIGHT The floor plan of the six-storey building – clad in a buff-coloured brick with a rug finish – is L-shaped, with wings protruding from both ends. The primary emphasis on the façade is horizontal, created by the stone bands above the first and fifth floors, and the protruding brick speed stripes at the corners and spanning the sixth floor. However, flourishes of Zigzag decoration adorn the building in key locations.

RIGHT The uppermost floor features outstanding Zigzag floral and geometric decoration. In this 1983 photo, the windows are still double-hung with multiple panes, while the decorative stone trim has been painted grey.

Manhattan Apartments

235 Cooper Street, Ottawa, Ontario
Werner Edgar Noffke, 1935

After arriving in Canada in 1902 and setting up a boot-making shop in what is now Ottawa's Chinatown district, Snear Miller began purchasing real estate before becoming an apartment developer in the late 1920s. His focus was the present-day neighbourhood of Centretown, in which low-rise apartment buildings had been erected for several decades, in part because of the 1911 opening of the nearby Victoria Memorial Museum and its surrounding green space.

Constructed in 1935 on the site of the former Protestant Orphan's Home, the Manhattan contained 35 apartments and shared a cinder block parking garage with its 24-unit cousin, the Royal York, to the north. The basement of the Royal York housed a suite of maids' rooms for tenants having live-in help. Snear helped attract tenants by assisting with their moving costs.

An article in the *Ottawa Evening Journal* praised the building: "The balconies for each suite, the doorways and windows are 'neo-modernistic' and while decidedly distinctive, are notable for good taste and dignity." It later notes: "the individual suites, small or large, are uniform in design, roomy where room is needed, compact where compactness means less work and ease in housekeeping…the bathrooms with built-in baths, showers and large well-fitted hand basins are models of what real bathrooms should be."

The building remains intact and well kept, with many interior features in their original condition.

RIGHT Step-back motifs and three-dimensional chevrons make this a dazzling Zigzag entrance. The wooden doors are original; the metal canopy – whose underside featured frosted-glass panels to illuminate the entry below – has been repainted since this photo was taken.

Manhattan Apartments

ABOVE The hexagonal, frosted-glass chandelier in the vestibule is an exceptional example of Zigzag styling.

TOP The multiple planes and step-back massing of its central portion – together with its dazzling entrance – make this four-storey, E-shaped block an Art Deco gem. Seen here in 1988, the balconies with their jazzy metal railings have since been replaced by modern French balconies. Notice the construction date proudly displayed atop the façade.

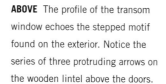

ABOVE The profile of the transom window echoes the stepped motif found on the exterior. Notice the series of three protruding arrows on the wooden lintel above the doors.

MIDDLE RIGHT Even the chrome-plated handle and push plate on the inside of the front door are embellished with Zigzag detailing.

RIGHT Multiple planes and a protruding series of chevrons embellish this decorative panel located atop the fluted pilasters that flank the front entry.

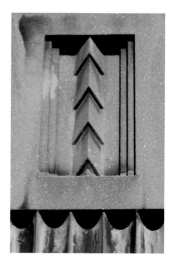

Park Square Apartments

425 Elgin Street, Ottawa, Ontario
Architect unknown, 1936

Between 1921 and 1941, the population of Ottawa grew by nearly 50 percent to reach 154,000 people, due in large part to the increasing size of the federal government's workforce. The Centretown neighbourhood's relative proximity to government offices made it an ideal location for apartment construction.

Snear Miller was not the only apartment developer active in Ottawa in the 1930s. In 1905, Wolf Shenkman arrived in Canada from Russia, and soon began building houses and apartments. He purchased property at the southeast corner of Park and Elgin Streets in 1934 for $6,000; two years later, his son Harold obtained a building permit to construct a three-storey apartment building that was estimated to cost $23,000.

The Park Square Apartments, with 13 units, was completed early the following year; a decade later, it sold for $55,000.

In 1974, the newly formed Centretown Citizens (Ottawa) Corporation unsuccessfully tried to purchase the building to turn it into non-profit housing; today, it remains a sought-after commercial apartment building.

LEFT This red-brick apartment building exhibits a careful balance of horizontal and vertical elements. On each of its three storeys, bands of contrasting dark-brown bricks, aligned with the larger windows, wrap around the building corners, while narrower bands of stacked brick rise upward between the smaller windows. The ground floor is accented by continuous recessed streamlines.

ABOVE The magnificent carved stone entrance displays primarily Streamlined styling. The smooth-faced building name, set in a bold Deco typeface, stands out from its rough-textured background. The round 'porthole' window – a common 1930s design element – is echoed by the semicircular windows in the front doors. Notice the grooved horizontal stone band directly above the doorway that curves over the window, neatly counterbalancing the strip of convex vertical stone 'rods' that top the entrance. A wonderful detail is the window's curved sliding sash.

Tweedsmuir Mansions

900 Park Boulevard, Victoria, British Columbia

William J. Semeyn, 1936

This upscale apartment building is situated in an ideal location; standing on the northern edge of Beacon Hill Park at the southern tip of the City of Victoria, it has a clear view of the Strait of Juan de Fuca and Washington's Olympic Mountains.

In August 1935, English-born Colin and Florence Forrest arrived in Victoria from Shanghai. They immediately hired local architect William J. Semeyn – notably, born in Holland and not in America or Britain – to design what is today considered one of Victoria's most impressive Streamlined Moderne structures.

Despite the Depression, the Forrests were confident about the future of the city, and invested significant funds in the building's construction. The Governor General of the day, Sir John Buchan, First Baron Tweedsmuir of Elsfield, granted them permission to name the apartment block Tweedsmuir Mansions.

It was an innovative apartment building, with its nine suites equipped with washing machines, extensive soundproofing, and oak floors. Some units had their own street entrance, while all shared a spacious parking area at the rear. It was the first apartment in Victoria built with a penthouse suite – the Forrest's new home.

A 1986 renovation replaced the smooth exterior stucco with a textured finish, somewhat compromising its sleek appearance. In 1988, a proposal to add eight new apartments was rejected by city council; three years later, however, two quite sympathetically designed units were added to its north wing. In 1995, it was converted from apartments to strata (condominium) ownership.

TOP The protruding curve on the third floor is echoed by the curved canopy over the front entrance, and the narrower two-storey sections flanking it. A series of nine vertical ribs adorn the face of the canopy, frame the central second-floor window, and terminate on the parapet.

BOTTOM This flat-roofed, stucco-clad Streamlined Moderne apartment building has a butterfly shaped plan, ensuring all units enjoy views of Beacon Hill Park. While curved walls accentuate the central entrance and the end apartments to the east, its squared corners feature chamfered wraparound windows. Notice the built-in balcony on the uppermost apartment to the right.

The Apartments of Willowdale Avenue, Montreal

A half-dozen Art Deco apartment buildings, built to house 1930s European immigrants, can be found just northwest of the University of Montreal, on the stretch of Willowdale Avenue in Montreal's Outremont district that projects into the eastern edge of Côte-des-Neiges.

It was not uncommon for these apartment buildings to have English names that evoked prestigious neighbourhoods or luxury residential properties in London or New York.

Three of these apartment buildings are profiled here. Each has a very distinctive entrance; otherwise, they exhibit subtle variations in their overall form, the placement of their balconies, and the variety of their decoration.

Canterbury Apartments
454 Willowdale Avenue, Montreal, Quebec
Maxwell Myron Kalman, 1937–38

On the 1938 City of Outremont building permit, James Melville Miller was listed as the architect for this 18-unit apartment building. However, architect Maxwell Myron Kalman disagreed, claiming that the property's owner, Moses Stern, had asked him in February 1937 to prepare plans and specifications for the building. After Kalman took legal action, Quebec's Superior Court sided with him, compelling Stern to pay him his fees for the building's design.

TOP The front entrance is an excellent example of Zigzag styling. The wooden doors contain slender vertical strips of glass that join together at right angles in the transom window. Multiple-plane, step-back stone piers flank the semicircular canopy and its gleaming chrome fascia. Chrome letters announce the building name in a wonderful 1930s typeface.

BOTTOM Slightly protruding bays with pairs of windows enliven the light-brown brick façade of the four-storey building. At either side of the façade, the wall is set further back to make room for rounded corner balconies. Notice the protruding brick speed stripes that stretch right across each floor; behind the aluminum storms, the original wooden-sash windows have horizontal panes, enhancing the building's streamlined appearance.

Anita Apartments

316 Willowdale Avenue, Montreal, Quebec

Patsy Colangelo, 1937–38

Thanks to its central stone pier, the Anita Apartments has one of the most distinctive façade treatments in the country. With a simple rectangular plan, it houses 13 apartments: four on each floor and one in the basement.

ABOVE A protruding stone pier climbs the entire height of the three-storey, red-brick façade. On each floor, stretches of dark-brown brick flanking frame the corner windows and wrap around the edges of the otherwise plain front façade. Projecting rectangular balconies on the second and third floors frame the central pier; the building's footprint is a rectangular block.

ABOVE The bold pattern of the glass panes in the front doors echoes the dynamism of the building's façade. The stone surround's bullnose corner is visible through the glass; its brass door handles feature a step-back profile.

ABOVE The front façade's vertical pier is a dazzling composition of stacked stone planes that emerge from a semicircular base. The narrowest top layer is adorned with a series of small flat 'buttons' that stretch the entire height of the pier. A horizontal stone band near the parapet containing corresponding recessed circles counterbalances this vertical element.

Modern Court Apartments

430 Willowdale Avenue, Montreal, Quebec

Patsy Colangelo, 1938

Architect Patsy Colangelo designed the four-storey Modern Court Apartments for Paul Asconi of Asconi Construction, who also owned the Anita Apartments. The H-shaped, 2,500-square-metre building houses 25 units – eight on each floor and one in the basement.

ABOVE The entrance to the three-storey, H-shaped building is significantly set back from the main façade. The building's Streamlined Moderne features include the continuous horizontal stone bands framing the tops and bottoms of the windows, the protruding speed stripes and glass blocks that wrap around the corners, and the sets of rounded-corner balconies on both sides of the entrance.

RIGHT The building's front doors are flanked by unique, half-round columns of glass block, and topped by a large glass-block transom. The doors themselves contain semi-circular windows with curved interior grilles.

The Apartments of St. Clair Avenue West, Toronto

The name Deer Park was given in the mid-1800s to the Heath family's 16-hectare estate at the northwest corner of the Third Concession Road (today's St. Clair Avenue) and Yonge Street. The name arose from the fact that very tame deer wandered the area, often being fed by guests at local hotels.

The Deer Park community – population 120 – first appeared in the city directory in 1885, and was annexed by the City of Toronto in 1908. Streetcar service westbound on St. Clair began in 1913, with several churches and schools being constructed in the neighbourhood over the next two decades.

By the 1930s, Deer Park had become a sought-after residential and shopping district, with commercial activity extending on St. Clair West about a block west of Yonge. The circumstances were ideal for the arrival of four 'high-class' apartment buildings. Three of these Streamlined Moderne buildings are profiled here; the fourth, London Terrace, was designed by Henry Douglas Llewellyn Morgan in 1938–39, but was later demolished.

The Park Lane

110 St. Clair Avenue West, Toronto, Ontario
Page & Steele, 1937

The nine-storey, dark-brown-brick Park Lane was described in its day as "the first of the modern style of large apartment house to be built in Toronto." Dominating its front façade is a deeply recessed entry bay that divides the U-shaped building into two identical wings, each of which is served by its own elevator. Each floor contains six apartments, two of which are two-bedroom units.

Matching sets of curved stairs leading to each wing's apartments face each other across the ground floor's elegant circular foyer. Of the ground level's six apartments, one is a bachelor unit to make room for a superintendent's office; the two outermost units at the rear have walkout patios. A penthouse apartment with a south-facing terrace is located atop each wing.

The Park Lane is well known for its connection to legendary yet eccentric Canadian classical pianist Glenn Gould, who lived in penthouse apartment #902 for the final two decades of his life. Gould slept and practised piano in his chronically messy apartment, but often dined at Fran's Restaurant, a 10-stool, 24-hour diner located a block to the east.

ABOVE Sheathed in dark-brown brick, the nine-storey Park Lane Apartments is an excellent example of Streamlined Moderne styling. Protruding brick speed stripes above and below the curved corner windows extend to each of the flanking windows, while stacks of three speed stripes grace the stretches of solid wall between them. The modern replacement windows lack the sophisticated proportions of the former multiple-pane units.

OPPOSITE This period photo of the Park Lane's foyer reveals its graceful attributes, including its circular cove ceiling and dazzling circular chandelier that featured frosted-glass fins and three circular discs. Notice the slightly curved steps leading to the western elevator, and the built-in curved seating and ashtray for visitors.

The Park Lane

The Fleetwood

64 St. Clair Avenue West, Toronto, Ontario

Henry John Chown, 1938

This six-storey, buff-brick apartment building is located a block east of the Park Lane. Construction of the $350,000 structure, featuring an H-shaped plan and containing 96 units of various sizes, began in April 1938.

ABOVE The protruding front bays of the six-storey Fleetwood have curved corners on both sides, but the windows themselves are smaller in size. Three protruding speed stripes wrap around the corners at each floor; decorated bands of stone enliven the parapet on each bay.

RIGHT In a period typeface, the Fleetwood's name is announced in large, freestanding chrome letters that follow the curve of the entrance canopy. Beneath, the original wooden doors feature step-back vertical windowpanes.

Whitehall Apartments

49 St. Clair Avenue West, Toronto, Ontario

Page & Steele, 1938

Located on the south side of St. Clair Avenue, the 40-unit, brick-clad building housed six one- and two-bedroom suites per floor plus six penthouse suites. The roof contained protected sun decks and badminton courts; parking garage facilities nearby meant that the entire basement was available to accommodate maids' quarters, laundry facilities 'with mechanical dryers,' lockers, and janitorial space.

The structure, built at a cost of $250,000, is still standing, but has lost much of its original grace. Specifically, its brick walls have been painted a tan colour; its multiple-plane, horizontally proportioned windows have been replaced by modern casements; its curved balconies have been enclosed in glass; and the ground floor now houses a sports bar.

RIGHT This period photo shows the eight-storey building shortly after it was completed. Its Streamlined Moderne features include the curved corners on the east and west façades that are contained on each floor by solid-wall curved balconies; the protruding speed stripes connecting pairs of windows and wrapping around the building's corners; and the step-back massing on the front façade. The name 'Whitehall' appeared in slender lower-case letters on the elegant curved canopy above the west side's front entrance. It has been considerably altered since it was constructed in 1938.

Park Lane Apartments

1360 Bernard Avenue West, Montreal, Quebec

Maxwell Myron Kalman, 1939

The village of Outremont – meaning 'beyond the mountain' – took its name, in 1875, from the home 'Outre-Mont' that was built in 1833 for the former Sheriff of Montreal, Louis-Tancrède Bouthillier. In 1927, it became the world's first city to clear its streets with the 'Sicard Snow Remover Snowblower' that was invented in Montreal two years earlier. Outremont remained a separate city until 2000, when it was amalgamated as a district of Montreal.

Located a few blocks east of the Outremont Metro station, the Park Lane was located on a stretch of Bernard Avenue that mostly contained apartments from the 1920s.

ABOVE Featuring primarily Zigzag styling, the Park Lane's front façade contains slightly protruding side wings. With its roughly rectangular floor plan, the beige-brick building houses five floors of apartments – three of which have rectangular metal balconies facing the street.

TOP The dazzling front entry includes a glass-block wall that surrounds the polished chrome doors. While green marble quarter-columns flank the doors, taller granite piers, topped by chrome strips, frame the overall entrance. Three multiple-plane protruding chrome bands rise behind the freestanding chrome letters spelling out the building's name in a bold Deco typeface. Notice the front doors' chamfered corners and the radiating lines etched in the glass.

RIGHT Tall strips of brick set at a 45-degree angle decorate the front of the façade's side bays. A simple pattern of slightly protruding bricks adds visual interest to the spandrels, while the balcony railings feature a circular detail.

FAR RIGHT Like many Deco-era apartment buildings, the front lobby features a geometric pattern in the terrazzo floor. Notice the star-shaped metal chandelier with exposed neon bulbs, and the interior panel of glass block.

Garden Court Apartments

1477 Bayview Avenue, Toronto, Ontario
Page & Steele, 1938–42

In what the *Toronto Star* described at the time as "one of the largest transactions in real estate in the Toronto districts this year [1938]," a young developer named Robert Jackson purchased a vacant lot, located some five kilometres northeast of the city's business centre, with the intention of building an innovative apartment project. The two-hectare property was located in the quintessential middle-class neighbourhood of Leaside, where single-family homes with a front and back yard sold for between $8,000 and $11,000.

Drawing upon examples found in Scandinavia and elsewhere, Jackson envisioned a residential complex that consisted of two- and three-storey buildings surrounding a large garden courtyard. Although less than 25 percent of the property was to be built upon, the project would provide for a total of 108 apartments in 14 separate buildings. Jackson – who had been associated since 1925 with his father's construction firm, Jackson-Lewis Company – hired the architectural firm of Page & Steele, experienced in apartment design, to bring his half-million-dollar project to life.

One of the most distinctive characteristics of Garden Court Apartments is the absence of internal hallways. For the two-storey buildings containing four apartments, the front door at street level serves the two units on the ground floor, while residents of the upper two units use a private staircase to access their apartments. (A similar set-up existed for the six apartments in the three-storey blocks; the ground-floor apartments that face Bayview Avenue on the front, and Berney Crescent at the rear, have their own individual front doors.) This unique configuration meant that each apartment had windows on opposite exterior walls, with some on three sides.

The basement of each block contained a storage room and laundry facilities to serve just its own units; some basements also included "winter recreation rooms" with ping-pong tables. Nearly 80 enclosed garages were provided along the north and south boundaries of the complex. From a construction perspective, Garden Court's innovations included the use of all-masonry walls, steel stairs and steel sash windows, plus reinforced concrete floor slabs that projected out to form the balconies, all of which were fireproof and durable.

The central courtyard, measuring nearly two-thirds of a hectare in size, was designed by the leading landscape

architecture firm of the day, H.B. Dunnington-Grubb. Its formal garden stepped down in a series of levels from Bayview Avenue to Berney Crescent, and was crisscrossed by flagstone and asphalt paths that led to each apartment entrance. These walkways were articulated by hedges of Alpine currant and Japanese yew, while weeping elm and mulberry trees further embellished this exceptional interior green space. Although two tennis courts and two sizeable children's playgrounds were intended to occupy the four corners of the property, only the tennis court at the northeast corner of the site was actually built.

A few changes have diminished the integrity of Garden Court since its construction nearly eight decades ago. Despite a campaign to preserve them, the original metal-sash windows were replaced in the early 2000s with modern white windows whose proportions match the originals, but with thicker mullions. At the same time, the original putty-coloured metal flashings were replaced with dark-brown metal, while the metal railings were also repainted dark brown. These alterations sadly compromised the original similarity of colour between the brickwork and metalwork. Nevertheless, Garden Court remains one of the most important Streamlined Moderne buildings in Canada.

In 1950, Garden Court was recognized with an inaugural Silver Award in the Massey Medals for Architecture program, created to celebrate excellence and heighten public awareness of architecture as an expression of Canadian cultural life.

ABOVE Garden Court is an outanding example of a Stream-lined Moderne low-rise, multi-unit residential complex. Seen here is the northern portion of its principal (west) façade, consisting of a three-storey block that's flanked by a two-storey block to the north. Compare the rounded-corner brick balconies on the taller block to the rectangular, metal-enclosed balcony on the smaller block. Notice the partial hip roof on the larger block that enhances the domestic character of the building.

Garden Court Apartments

ABOVE This courtyard view, photographed prior to the replacement of the windows and metal flashing, illustrates the skillful integration of the landscaping with the built form. Notice the protruding brick speed stripes that frame the windows and mark the building corners; the chimney in the two-storey corner unit served a main-floor fireplace.

RIGHT Behind the tall, glass-block window of this west-facing block is a staircase and series of landings that serve its individual apartments. The curved balconies and decorative railing atop the entrance enhance its Streamlined character.

TOP LEFT The protruding brick speed stripes are especially evident in this view of the main Bayview Avenue entrance after a light snowfall.

LEFT The balustrade on the staircase in a two-storey unit features a trio of railing bars, while a three-tier step-back crowns the newel post.

ABOVE Three planes of brick surround a window that illuminates the staircase in a two-storey block. Notice how the metal window sash contains three horizontally proportioned panes.

Athlone Apartments

895 Academy Close, Victoria, British Columbia
Birley, Wade & Stockdill, 1940

Due to the region's gentle climate that permitted the use of flat roofs and stucco finishes, Victoria has a significant concentration of Streamlined Moderne residential buildings.

Located just a few blocks north of the Tweedsmuir Mansions built four years earlier, the two-storey Athlone Apartments housed 12 one-bedroom suites, accessed from three separate stair towers. And like its neighbour, the Athlone was named after Canada's Governor General of the day, Alexander Cambridge, the First Earl of Athlone. All units back onto Southgate Street, with views of Beacon Hill Park. To the north side of the building is a garage with seven bays.

Formerly a rental apartment building, occupants now become legal partners who jointly own the Athlone, making for closer relationships with neighbours and fewer resales.

ABOVE The slightly taller, rounded-corner stair tower dominates the central portion of the façade. The inner corners of the flanking bays are more gently rounded; the horizontally proportioned windowpanes – together with the wraparound windows in the end units – contribute to the building's Streamlined Moderne character.

RIGHT Awning-type sashes enhancing natural ventilation top the leaded-glass windows in the central stair tower. A rising concrete wall wraps around the curved steps leading up to the front entry. The horizontal bands framing the entrance canopy's rounded-corner fascia match those that wrap around the parapet of the front façade. The building's stucco has been returned to its original white colour since this photo was taken in 1992.

Athlone Apartments

330 – 19th Avenue Southwest, Calgary, Alberta

Fordyce & Stevenson, 1940

Prominent Calgary businessman Arthur Cumming went against the grain in 1940 when he decided to build a luxury apartment building in the city's Mission district, which was then slowly devolving from an upper-class to lower-middle-class neighbourhood. By naming it the Athlone Apartments (after the sitting Governor General), Cumming likely hoped to make his new Art Deco–style building seem more prestigious.

At 46 suites over three floors, the Athlone was Mission's largest and most modern apartment building at the time. Like most other brick structures in the neighbourhood, it was constructed over a wood frame, then faced with brick. Inside, the suites featured electrical appliances, oak and linoleum floors, venetian blinds in all the windows, indirect lighting, and dual-type faucets – with mechanical stoppers instead of rubber plugs in the kitchen sinks. A Moderne-style glass globe illuminated the main stairs, while the interior corridor walls featured rounded corners.

Besides Cumming himself, one of the early occupants of the Athlone was World War I flying ace Captain Fred McCall, after whom Calgary's present airport was first named. In 1987, the Athlone was renamed Leah Manor, but returned to its original name some years later.

ABOVE Two stories tall with a raised basement, the façade of the symmetrical, U-shaped apartment building is clad in two colours of red brick. The Streamlined Moderne wings feature continuous concrete lintels above the first- and second-floor windows, and lighter-red-brick speed stripes stretching across the entire façade. The horizontal emphasis continues in the recessed grooves in the foundation wall.

LEFT The main façade's upper-floor windows are elaborately decorated. Beneath the stone sill (in this case, damaged) is a low-relief stone panel containing a series of overlapping discs framed by a pair of convex vertical ribs, in turn flanked by recessed speed stripes. Above the window is a series of curved 'shields,' on top of which is a panel of brick in a herringbone pattern.

TOP The central portion of the façade, set well back from the street, features both Zigzag and Streamlined Moderne details. In the middle are three slightly protruding brick piers that draw attention to the bold stone-framed entrance. By contrast, protruding brick speed stripes frame the windows. The entrance portal, which contains subtle multiple-plane detailing, frames a glass-block wall that surrounds the front doors, helping illuminate the foyer.

Single-Family Homes

Lawren Harris House

2 Ava Crescent, Toronto, Ontario
Alexandra Biriukova, 1930

As the grandson of one of the founders of Canadian farm equipment manufacturing giant Massey-Harris, Brantford, Ontario–born Lawren Harris had the financial means to pursue his love in painting. Celebrated for his talents as a landscape artist, the founder of the Group of Seven was interested in philosophy, later becoming a member of the International Theosophical Society. Less well known is his fascination with modern architecture.

When he set out to build a home for his family in Toronto, Harris turned to his Russian-born friend and architect, Alexandra Biriukova.

Biriukova had fled Russia in 1914 with an architectural degree earned in Petrograd; she went on to complete a post-graduate degree in Rome. In 1929, she moved to Toronto to join her artist sister, and soon after completed the interior design of a Russian Orthodox Church in the city. By this point, at age 35, Biriukova was well versed in the styles of contemporary European architecture that were of interest to Harris.

Her design involved a three-storey central block that was flanked by a pair of symmetrical, two-storey wings. Situated on a very deep lot, the house was set back some 30 metres from the curved street, and positioned at a southwest-facing angle to allow for a driveway that reached the built-in, two-car garage at the rear.

Inside the front door was a two-storey, oval-shaped foyer with a grand semicircular staircase opposite the door. Radiating out from the foyer was a series of variously shaped rooms, all with tall, metal-sash windows and high ceilings. To the left was the octagonal dining hall and adjoining kitchen; to the right was the large rectangular living room that led into a five-sided library. Bathed in natural light, these rooms were ideal for hanging paintings by Harris and his friends. The upper floors contained three bedrooms, three baths, a study, and an outdoor terrace over the garage.

Since the home's construction, additions have been built at the rear, the distinctive landscaping altered and front-entry gate removed.

Although Biriukova was the first woman to join the Ontario Association of Architects in 1931, the Lawren Harris house proved to be her last commission. Whether due to gender or racial discrimination, or the effects of the Depression, she abandoned architecture and spent the rest of her life as a hospital nurse.

ABOVE Framing the front entrance gate were twin piers crowned with stunning metal carriage lamps whose frosted panels were embellished with pine-needle motifs. The hinged gate was adorned with a decorative '2,' marking the home's address. The curves in the gate's balusters matched those in the French balcony beneath the tall central window.

ABOVE Seen here in 1995, the stucco-covered, flat-roofed former home of Group of Seven painter Lawren Harris was a sophisticated blend of Art Deco and Modern styling. Matching, two-storey wings with chamfered corners flank the three-storey central block containing the front entrance. A series of recessed multiple planes surround the central arched window. The elegant front gate and landscaping alongside the driveway and walkway have been removed.

RIGHT Pine needles were a consistent decorative motif across the home's exterior; here they decorate the cast-metal spandrel panel on the tall central window.

Cormier House

1418 Pine Avenue, Montreal, Quebec
Ernest Cormier, 1930–31

Arguably the finest Art Deco residence in all of Canada was designed and built in 1930–31 by Ernest Cormier – French Canada's 'renaissance man.'

In creating this home for himself, Cormier drew upon his diverse training and talents: a civil engineering degree from the *École polytechnique* in Montreal; studies in architecture, painting, sculpture, and watercolour at the prestigious *École des beaux-arts* in Paris; and three years designing reinforced concrete structures at a French engineering firm.

When architects design their own home, they are free to consider ideas that they might otherwise be unable to explore for a conventional client. In the case of Maison Cormier, the varied architectural styles and the degree of sophistication in their execution is exceptional – so much so that the house was awarded the Royal Architectural Institute of Canada's Gold Medal in 1932.

Dramatically situated on a steeply sloping lot on the south side of Pine Avenue, the seemingly single-storey building facing the street is actually five stories tall on its southeast-facing rear façade, overlooking downtown Montreal. While the house is attached to a taller, more traditional building to the west, each of its remaining façades is styled differently: the front is Art Deco, the east side is mostly symmetrical but unadorned, while the rear is clearly International Style with a Mediterranean feel. Built of reinforced concrete, the exterior materials are similarly differentiated: the Pine Avenue façade is artificial granite, while the side and rear walls are finished with stucco.

The top floor facing Pine Avenue (level five) contains the home's principal rooms: the kitchen and pantry, the dining room, a cloakroom and powder room, an outdoor terrace, and the pièce de resistance – Cormier's spacious studio. Measuring more than five metres wide, over eight metres long and well over seven metres in height, the studio is illuminated by windows on three sides, with the entrance to the room axially opposite the dramatic marble fireplace.

One floor below is the master bedroom with an adjoining dressing room and closet, as well as a second bedroom, two

rooms for the maid, the grocery and wine cellar – plus the other essential space: the windowless library complete with a corner fireplace. Level three is occupied by the housekeeper's living room and kitchen, two bedrooms and bathrooms, plus storage. The next floor down contains the heating system, vegetable cellar, and incinerator; outdoors is an herb garden. On the bottom floor, level with Redpath Street, is the home's two-car garage.

Cormier lived in the house until 1975, the same year that the Government of Quebec declared it a historic monument. Shortly after Cormier's death in 1980, Prime Minister Pierre Trudeau purchased Maison Cormier and lived there until his passing in 2000. The home remains in the Trudeau family.

ABOVE The north-facing front façade, clad in artificial granite, consists of two distinct blocks, the taller of which is dominated by the large studio window. Atop this window are three decorative vertical bands, adorned with floral motifs; below is a heavy stone planter with carved bunches of grapes. Notice how the window's horizontal mullions are aligned with the wall's mortar joints to create an uninterrupted lateral effect that contrasts with the series of subtle vertical planes flanking the opening.

FAR LEFT The entrance to the house is quintessential Art Deco. A series of receding multiple planes frame the solid-wood front door, which is protected by a half-octagonal stone canopy that matches the stoop below. Narrow incised bands of convex ribs flank the modest opening in the door.

LEFT Above the front door is a carving of a clothed muse holding a model of the central tower of the University of Montreal (see page 98), which was concurrently being built on the opposite side of Mount Royal.

Cormier House

ABOVE LEFT The site's steep slope is evident in this period photo of the east façade. Below the top floor, the wall is finished in roughly trowelled stucco; the windows are arranged in a generally symmetrical fashion that was dictated in part by the home's interior layout. The stone from the home's excavation was used for walkways in the garden, while the rather whimsical stone turret at the rear contained a staircase linking the terrace to the garage. On the front façade, notice the uninterrupted horizontal configuration of studio window's original mullions.

ABOVE RIGHT This is one of the photos that Cormier commissioned shortly after the home was completed. Alternating bands of beige and orange wood-veneer wallpaper create a Streamlined counterpoint to the imposing, polished-marble fireplace with its step-back and multiple-plane detailing. The similarly coloured terrazzo floor is patterned in interlocking circles, framed by slender copper borders and tiny dark marble squares. The studio's unique entry space, directly opposite the fireplace, is defined by four giant marble columns, echoing the entrance hall at the University of Montreal. Beyond lies the semicircular staircase to the library below. Cormier designed much of the home's furniture, including the black marble table and stools in the centre of the studio, and its geometric club chairs executed in orange leather.

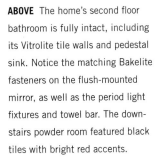

ABOVE The home's second floor bathroom is fully intact, including its Vitrolite tile walls and pedestal sink. Notice the matching Bakelite fasteners on the flush-mounted mirror, as well as the period light fixtures and towel bar. The downstairs powder room featured black tiles with bright red accents.

UPPER MIDDLE Haig family members were summoned to the dinner table with this elegant Streamlined gong.

ABOVE The streamlining continues on the curved, multiple-plane top of the staircase sidewall. Lath-and-plaster construction made it feasible to build curved walls and openings.

ABOVE Curved walls and bullnose corners were employed in various locations on the ground floor, including this entry area for the powder room. Notice how the bottom of the main staircase, including the railing and baseboard, follows the curve of the wall.

Arnold House

279 Glasgow Street, Kitchener, Ontario
William Arnold (designer and builder), 1937

In the Kitchener, Ontario neighbourhood of Westmount, various homebuilders constructed houses during the interwar period for bank managers, lawyers, newspapermen, factory superintendents, and other professionals.

One such builder was William Arnold, who purchased four lots on Glasgow Street, a few blocks east of the Westmount Golf and Country Club. On three of the lots he built conventional two-storey, Tudor-style houses; for the fourth property, he took a different approach and constructed the neighbourhood's first modern home that we now describe as Streamlined Moderne. Its distinctive features included a terrazzo floor in the vestibule, green laminated cupboards and an oversize window in the kitchen, plus two large curved walls on the ground floor.

Arnold lived in the house until 1947, after which it was sold to a stockbroker, and subsequently to a Kitchener city councillor. In 1982, it was designated as a heritage house under the Ontario Heritage Act.

TOP This builder-designed two-storey house incorporates key features of the Streamlined Moderne style, including wraparound corner windows with horizontally proportioned panes, and protruding stone bands that stretch across the white stucco façade. Its hipped roof, however, is unusual for such a streamlined structure.

MIDDLE A flat roof and a large bow window with horizontally proportioned panes enclose this southwest-facing alcove off the living room. A rear-facing room has a similar glazed wall with square panes of glass.

RIGHT This distinctive front-door surround is made of poured-in-place concrete. A series of planes topped with vertical grooves and curved corners flank the stepped-profile rectangular frame. Curiously, the underside of the lintel features a decorative ogee detail. Notice the horizontal mullions in the porthole window beside the door.

Second G.D. Loane House

1858 Abbott Street, Kelowna, British Columbia

Robert Lyon, 1937

Thanks to the health of the fruit industry in the Okanagan Valley, the City of Kelowna weathered the Great Depression reasonably well. Residential construction flourished, with a number of higher-end houses – including this Streamlined Moderne masterpiece – being built near the eastern shore of Okanagan Lake, just south of downtown.

Well-known Kelowna businessman Gordon Donald Loane, who managed W.W. Loane Hardware and Paints, commissioned architect Robert Lyon – whose public buildings are profiled on pages 64 and 78 – to design the family's second home. (Their previous home was built for them in 1933, in the traditional Arts and Crafts style.) Beyond the usual kitchen, dining room, and living room with a fireplace, the house's main floor contained a small master bedroom and bathroom, plus a second bedroom.

Upstairs were two more bedrooms and a small bathroom, while the basement contained a tool room, cold room, furnace room, and a large playroom.

The Second G.D. Loane House was designated a Municipal Heritage Site in 2004. A set of design guidelines helps ensure that new development in the Abbott Street Heritage Area is compatible with the existing legacy of homes in the neighbourhood.

In 2007, the home's current owners began a significant addition to the house that seamlessly complements the original structure; their efforts were recognized with a 2010 Central Okanagan Heritage Society Award in the New Construction Compatible with Its Heritage Surroundings category.

BELOW Containing two floors and a basement, this wood-frame house finished with lightly textured white stucco is an outstanding example of the Streamlined Moderne style, as demonstrated by its asymmetrical yet balanced massing, its corner windows on two floors, and the curved canopy over the front door that echoes the curved wall on the second floor. Notice the series of bullnose corners on the stepped stucco 'shelf' facing the front door. When it was built, the flashing at the roofline was lighter in colour, and the second floor railing was not present.

Second G.D. Loane House

RIGHT The front entrance's curved concrete steps match the shape of the canopy above. The house's interior doors have the same horizontally proportioned panes of glass as the front door. A period photo indicates that all windows on the front façade were operable casements.

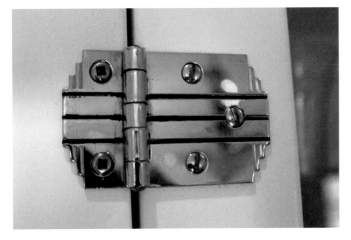

ABOVE This view of the western façade reveals the stepped profile of the main chimney. The curved canopy and one-storey block to the rear were part of the addition project that began in 2007.

TOP RIGHT The entire portion of the house visible in this photo was added to the original dwelling – an excellent example of a compatible renovation.

MIDDLE RIGHT Vertical grooves and a rounded profile embellished the back plate of the polished chrome doorknobs.

MIDDLE FAR RIGHT The plaster wall framing the door opening features a bullnose treatment. Notice the careful curved detailing in the baseboard.

RIGHT As tiny a detail as the hinges on cupboard doors were adorned with three incised speed stripes and subtle step-backs.

Dr. L.A. Miller Residence

13108 Churchill Crescent NW, Edmonton, Alberta
George Prudham (designer and builder), 1938

The development of Edmonton's Glenora neighbourhood, in which this house is located, began with landowner James Carruthers. In 1909, he struck an agreement with the City of Edmonton that, if it extended streetcar service to this area, he would build a bridge across the ravine that separated the neighbourhoood from the rest of the city. Determined to ensure that the area would become an upscale community, he instituted the Carruthers Caveat, which stipulated that at least $3,500 needed to be spent in constructing any house in the neighbourhood. Part of Glenora's appeal lay in the fact that it was upwind of downtown, ensuring it enjoyed better air quality than similar districts to the east.

On April 20, 1937, a building permit was filed for the construction of this Streamlined Moderne house, which was first occupied by Dr. L.A. Miller, who had moved to Canada with his family in 1899 from Hungary. His brother, Abe Miller, was a municipal and provincial politician in the 1950s.

TOP RIGHT Thanks to the continuous incised speed stripes above the second floor, the corner windows, and the curved canopy and stretch of wall beside the front door, this two-storey, stucco house clearly fits the definition of Streamlined Moderne. Most of the windows are in groups of three; the room above the one-car garage was added later.

RIGHT Streamlined features abound inside the home, such as this curved wall leading into the kitchen. Other examples include curved window valances with incised speed stripes, a built-in china cabinet with circular trim, and the rounded corner on the sidewall of the main staircase.

FAR RIGHT The chevron pattern of the glazing in the storm door is matched on the mostly solid main door. The leaded-glass window to the left illuminates the curved vestibule.

Rashotte House

139 Victoria Street South, Tweed, Ontario

The Rashotte family (design and construction); William Arthur Watson (consulting architect), 1938–39

In the mid-1800s, the colony of Upper Canada gave sizeable tracts of land to lumber traders and other brave souls who would come and start a new life in the harsh wilderness. One area populated in this fashion was Tweed – a small community situated on Stoco Lake, some 40 kilometres north of Belleville, Ontario – that was endowed with good forests.

Members of the French-speaking Rajotte family moved to Tweed in the 1850s, after the raging spring waters of the St. Lawrence River destroyed their farm near Sorel, Quebec. (They chose Tweed because some of the men in the family had previously spent winters working at lumber camps in the area.) On their 40-hectare plot of land, they built log cabins and cleared the land to plant their first crops. The children of these early families were educated in English, and since the schoolteacher had trouble pronouncing French names, the Rajotte name was anglicized to Rashotte.

On July 7, 1937, Joseph Raphael Rashotte – son of the prominent local builder Paul Rashotte – married Marjorie Quinn, whose family ran the local department store. They paid $400 for a building lot on the western shore of Stoco Lake, and demolished the house that stood on it. By their second anniversary, they were settled into this new home that they had jointly designed (with oversight from Belleville-based architect William Arthur Watson); father Paul helped with its construction. They lived in the three-bedroom house for more than four decades.

To this day, the Rashotte name remains associated with the lumber and building business in Tweed.

TOP Designed by its owners, this two-storey Streamlined Moderne stucco house stands out from the red-brick or clapboard house elsewhere in town. Dominating its façade is a full-height curved window that, in this 1980s photo, still retains its original metal frame with clear glass panes. Other streamlined features include the corner windows, the small octagonal window, and the continuous protruding molding near the roofing.

ABOVE As seen in this 2008 photo, the clear glass in the curved window has been replaced by glass block, the double-hung corner windows have been updated, and the garage converted into living space.

Hambly House

170 Longwood Road North, Hamilton, Ontario
Edward Glass (designer), 1939

The three-bedroom Hambly House – built in 1939 for Jack Hambly and located on a corner lot in Hamilton's planned suburb of Westdale – stood boldly apart from its Tudor Revival neighbours.

The nautically inspired design of the house is attributed to Edward Glass, who was not a registered architect. (Glass was known to be a clerk at a downtown Hamilton shoe store, but in 1937 was listed as the designer of a residence in nearby Burlington.)

Inside the home, the bathroom fixtures were pale green with colour-coordinated wall tiles; the kitchen boasted brown plywood cupboards, grey Formica countertops, and red linoleum tiles. Not surprising for the period, the styling of the basement family room was 'National Park–Rustic,' with concrete walls shaped and painted to resemble a log cabin, complete with faux knots.

Fast-forward to 2010, when German-born Martin Hering and Nadine Kadri purchased the house from its long-time owner, and invested a considerable sum to restore it to its original condition. Their efforts were rewarded the next year with an Urban Design and Architecture Award and a Heritage Property Conservation Award. Within a year however, Hering put the home on the market, and subsequently returned to Europe. Sadly, the house was insufficiently maintained, suffering water damage and mould growth in the damp summer of 2013.

At this point, another couple saw the home's potential. Under the direction of a local architect, the house was stripped-down to its original skeleton, the ground floor opened up, the stucco replaced with a comparable modern finish, and the windows upgraded while retaining their original proportions and blue exterior colour. The most dramatic change was the addition of a glazed second floor, which housed a new family room and master bedroom. Thankfully, the rustic cabin basement was not altered.

TOP The horizontally proportioned glass panes in the windows and front door framed the daylight entering the home's interior in this 2011 photo. Notice the speed stripe detailing on the wooden fireplace mantel, which was flanked by built-in bookcases.

MIDDLE RIGHT Seen here in 2011, the one-storey, concrete-block home literally sparkled on sunny days, on account of the extra cement and quartz in its stucco finish. Its Streamlined Moderne attributes included the large curve topping the façade's cutaway corner; its prominent step-back front door surround; and its nautical-style curved metal railing. The landscaping was designed to evoke the impression of a ship cresting a wave.

BOTTOM RIGHT The 2015 renovation added a slightly set back glazed second storey, complete with a matching curved corner, and revamped the home's landscaping.

Halton House

33 Sylvan Lane, Victoria, British Columbia
John Hanzlik (architect and builder), 1941

The founding of the Victoria Golf Club and the Royal Victoria Yacht Club in the 1890s reflected the popularity of the Oak Bay district, endowed with sweeping tidewater beaches and granite hills. Incorporated in 1906, the municipality was soon served by sewers and waterpipes, ushering in a period of single-family residential development. By 1941, the community's population had risen to 9,000 people.

One of these houses was built by Jack Halton and his wife. Excited about the opportunity to enjoy the spectacular view across the Strait of Juan de Fuca to Washington State's Olympic Mountains, they purchased a steeply sloping piece of property consisting of solid rock. Four construction companies declined the opportunity to build on such a challenging site before the Haltons discovered John Hanzlik. Born in Poland and at that point in his mid-sixties, this architect and builder had come to Victoria from California and had travelled widely in Europe. For him, the project was a chance to build a unique home that capitalized on the property's hilltop location.

This Streamlined Moderne home's unique features include a stylized 'H' in the entrance foyer's linoleum floor, a 'floating' built-in china cabinet with glass pocket doors, a black toilet and sink in the original bathroom, and an octagonal porthole window that ventilated the master-bedroom closet. Former Canadian Prime Minister Lester Pearson was once photographed in the living room of the house.

Unable to afford to heat the home, the Haltons moved out after only three years. A recent owner added several bedrooms and a bathroom, but restored many of its original elements. The home was listed on Victoria's Community Heritage Register in 2008.

TOP A curved canopy above the front entrance protruded from the curved wall. Notice the subtle wave pattern in the stucco at the cornice.

RIGHT Clad in white stucco, the flat-roof Streamlined Moderne house consisted of two main floors and a basement with a low ceiling. Its wood-frame structure was built atop a concrete slab cantilevered out from the rock slope. The front of the main-floor façade featured two rounded corners; the upper floor had wraparound casement windows plus an octagonal porthole window. The rear of the house had exceptional ocean views. The steep site necessitated a winding stone staircase from the street-level garage up to the home's front entrance.

Smith Residence

18 Marcelle Avenue, Corner Brook, Newfoundland
W. George Smith (designer and builder), 1950

Thanks to the prevalence of timber on the west coast of Newfoundland, the Reid Newfoundland Company – the island's dominant landowner, railway, and ferry operator – teamed up with the Newfoundland government in 1923 to construct a large pulp and paper mill, along with the supporting infrastructure and town site, on the south shore of Humber Arm. Corner Brook Pulp and Paper Limited produced its first roll of paper two years later; in 1938, Bowater, a large British paper company, purchased the mill as it sought to establish a presence in the lucrative North American market.

One of the engineers at Bowater was W. George Smith, who built two houses on adjacent lots in an older Corner Brook neighbourhood. Smith must have been exposed to prevailing design trends, since the appearance of the homes embodied many attributes of the Streamlined Moderne style.

As a precaution in light of growing international tensions, he equipped each home's basement with a sizeable bomb shelter, constructed of concrete walls, ceilings, and stairs.

TOP RIGHT Exhibiting the principles of Streamlined Moderne design, the nearly symmetrical, two-storey, concrete-block house is painted white with black trim. It features a flat roof, rounded corners, and prominent horizontal lines; a rounded-corner canopy over the front door boasts tiny, multiple-plane dentils and is supported by slender round columns. Glass block is used extensively on the façade, including the sizeable curved windows and the rectangular band surrounding the front entrance. The interior walls and trim echoed the exterior curves.

RIGHT Although the central portion of the façade is slightly taller than the side wing, they both contain equal-height, glass-block curved windows. Notice how the dimensions of the square glass blocks match the height of the concrete blocks, enhancing the sense of sleek horizontality.

LIFE AS A
SHOPPER

Like today, shopping was an integral part of life for Canadians during the interwar period. This chapter first explores the well-known department stores, where products large and small were on offer, plus local independent shops, where the various necessities of life could be purchased. Next are showrooms and exhibition halls that displayed the newest and greatest items of interest to consumers and businesses alike. The chapter finishes with a sampling of both magnificent and more down-to-earth places in which to enjoy a meal.

T. Eaton Company 'College Street' Store

444 Yonge Street, Toronto, Ontario

Ross & Macdonald; Sproatt & Rolph (associates); interiors by René Cera (staff architect), 1919–28

Plenty has been written elsewhere about the history of Eaton's: the humble beginnings of Irish-born Timothy as a merchant, the launch of its mail-order catalogue business, its expansion into a coast-to-coast retail chain, and its unfortunate demise in the late 1990s. This story focuses on the company's glory days, when, in today's parlance, it was a fully integrated business that operated as manufacturer, distributor, and marketer; it described itself as the largest retail organization in the British Empire. Eaton's was Canada's trendsetter for women – and families at large – in all aspects of daily life.

The ultimate expression of the company's heyday was its ambitious plan to construct a full-block edifice topped by a 36-storey skyscraper in the new upscale shopping district that it sought to establish at Yonge and College Streets in Toronto. The design was the combined work of Montreal-based architects Ross & Macdonald, and Sproatt & Rolph of Toronto. The new building, at the southwest corner of the intersection, would house the company's offices and flagship store, augmenting its longstanding downtown store a few blocks south at Yonge and Queen. The arrival of the Depression meant that only the seven-storey base of the complex would be constructed; it opened on October 30, 1930.

The structure's exterior – constructed with Canadian-sourced materials – was Stripped Classical; in the words of one trade journal, it combined "the spirit of modernity with classical motifs." The store's state-of-the-art interior – including its elevators, lighting, and display cases – was designed by René Cera, a French-born, Beaux-Arts-trained architect who had moved to Canada in 1928 to head up the company's Architectural Design department.

The ground level – with warm grey marble walls and travertine marble floors – housed a variety of merchandise. 'The Elevator Arcade,' stretching along Yonge Street, contained home furnishings, tablewares, sewing machines, electrical fixtures, plus pianos and radios. The College Street portion consisted of 'Specialty Shops' – a series of small outlets selling children's and adult's clothing, perfumes, antiques, and a bookstore. The main floor even featured 'The Thrift Home' – a fully furnished model bungalow.

LEFT This 1928 rendering presented the T. Eaton Company's vision for its new headquarters. It would have exceeded 200 metres in height and contained over 460,000 square metres of floor space. Only the seven-storey base of the complex was actually built.

The second floor focused on home furnishings, and boasted a sculpture court at the centre of the fine arts department, together with a photography studio and beauty salon offering two-dozen treatment rooms. On the third floor were Oriental and Persian rugs; besides selling contemporary and period furniture, the fourth floor contained the 'Ideal Ontario Home' – the result of an architectural competition boasting a $2,500 first prize. The fifth floor featured the 'Gallery of Antiques and Reproductions,' plus a series of period rooms. The spaces on the legendary Seventh Floor – the Round Room Restaurant and Eaton Auditorium – will be profiled in upcoming pages.

The 1977 opening of the Eaton Centre at Yonge and Dundas Streets – designed by Eberhard Zeidler – led to the closure of both the College Street and Queen Street stores. The ground floor of the College Street store was later renovated to become the series of boutique shops known as College Park, while all the upper floors – except the Seventh Floor – became office space.

T. Eaton Company 'College Street' Store

ABOVE Of the initial scheme, only this seven-storey block – together with a lower-height portion that stretched south to Hayter Street, and a one-storey section west to Bay Street (since demolished) – was actually built. The Stripped Classical structure is clad in Tyndall limestone from Eaton's quarry in Manitoba, with brown granite from Gananoque, Ontario, framing the large, ground-floor shop windows. Giant fluted pilasters separate the sets of recessed windows on the upper floors.

TOP RIGHT The seventh-floor attic is set back from the main façade. The detailing on the entablature is quintessential Stripped Classical, with stylized floral forms adorning the pilaster capitals, roundels, and rectangular carved panels, as well as the aluminum cornice trim.

RIGHT The treatment of the Hayter Street doors hints at the level of detail found throughout the ground-floor interior. The pink marble walls are accented with Canadian-made Monel metal trim, while the vertically oriented grill-work above the doors is repeated in other areas of the building.

RIGHT A range of Zigzag geometric and stylized floral motifs are found in the Monel metal trim around the Hayter Street entrance.

ABOVE This period photo of the lighting-fixture department showcases the spaciousness of the ground floor and its elegant merchandising. Notice the giant decorative urns and the sleek chandelier.

Western Extension, Simpson's Department Store

Bay Street at Richmond Street West, Toronto, Ontario

Chapman & Oxley, 1928–29

Scottish-born Robert Simpson arrived in Canada in 1855, and within three years had established his own dry-goods business in Newmarket, Ontario, north of Toronto. After an 1870 fire, he moved to Toronto and set up shop on Yonge Street, a short distance north of Queen Street, where there were more than a dozen similar businesses. 'R. Simpson, Dry Goods' differentiated itself from its competitors – including the T. Eaton Company – by distributing colourful 'dodgers' (flyers) to city homes. Nine years after Eaton's had done so, the company published its first mail-order catalogue in 1893, attracting customers across the country.

The quadrupling of Toronto's population between 1871 and 1896 prompted Simpson, in 1894, to move the business to larger premises at the southwest corner of Yonge and Queen. After a fire levelled this new structure, Simpson opened a rebuilt, fully fireproof, red sandstone building two years later that stretched from Queen Street a full block south to Richmond Street. After Simpson's untimely death the next year, three Toronto businessmen purchased Robert Simpson Company Limited from the family for $135,000.

As a result of ongoing growth – and in response to the new Eaton's store at Yonge and College (see previous story) – Simpson's undertook a significant expansion to its flagship location, extending the building along Richmond westward all the way to Bay Street. This nine-storey, $4-million addition (planned to rise an additional 11 floors) expanded the store's sales space, and featured the new Arcadian Court on the top two floors. This prestigious restaurant – able to serve 1,300 patrons between its main floor and its men's-only mezzanine level – was reportedly the largest department store restaurant in the world. Offering quality food at reasonable prices, Arcadian Court sought to lure lunchtime diners away from the Georgian Room at Eaton's Queen Street store, the new Round Room Restaurant at Eaton's College Street (see page 202), and the Imperial Room at the nearby Royal York Hotel. The Arcadian Court also played host to other events, including Canada's first-ever auto show, and early radio broadcasts by the Toronto Symphony Orchestra. In 1972, the company's name was changed to Simpsons in response to Quebec's French-language issues.

The company slogan, "You'll enjoy shopping at Simpson's," lasted until the company was purchased by the Hudson's Bay Company in 1978. The Yonge and Queen location kept the Simpsons name until 1991, and the building remains the country's largest department store.

Arcadian Court, rechristened The Arcadian, reopened in 2012 after a year-long renovation, and is a popular venue for weddings and other events.

ABOVE Zigzag-style detailing embellishes the upper floors of the building, including wave-themed stone spandrels, plus floral motifs crowned with overlapping triangles above the ninth-floor windows. Notice the multiple-plane stone strips with sculpted volutes that decorate the top of each slender brick pier.

RIGHT Six storeys of smooth, reddish-brown brick rise above a three-storey stone base, as seen in this 1980s view of the southwest corner of the building.

ABOVE This 2011 view of the main Bay Street entrance showcases the elegant grillwork that enlivened the building's base. The use of arches on the addition's entrances may have been a nod to the original 1896 building. Floral and geometric motifs provide a backdrop for the large emblem containing the initials 'RSC.'

ABOVE The Toronto Symphony Orchestra prepares for a radio broadcast from the eighth-floor Arcadian Court in this period photograph. The Court's 12- metre-high ceiling contained three sizeable circular skylights; the artificial lighting included four giant Sabino chandeliers and eight tulip-shaped wall sconces. The wrought-iron railings on the mezzanine level featured motifs similar to the exterior metalwork. The space's original colours were beige and turquoise.

S.S. Kresge Company
43 King Street East, Hamilton, Ontario
Garnet Andrew McElroy, 1930

Born in Pennsylvania in 1867 to Swiss-born farmers, Sebastian Spering Kresge worked at odd jobs such as delivering groceries, teaching, and keeping bees before becoming a travelling salesman. He spent the next eight years selling hardware and tinware to New England merchants, including his future competitor Frank Woolworth.

At age 30, S.S. took his $8,000 of savings and, with a partner, purchased two five-and-dime stores in Detroit and Memphis. A decade later, after buying out his partner, Kresge incorporated his company as the S.S. Kresge Company; by 1929, the organization operated nearly 600 stores across America. Although he was very frugal personally, Kresge was a generous employer, offering such benefits as paid holidays and profit-sharing.

Canada's first Kresge store arrived in 1929; a year later, the company opened its twenty-second outlet in Hamilton – the country's largest single-floor variety store at the time. Additions were constructed to the north and east in 1948, but after 64 years of business, the Kresge store was closed in 1994.

Although somewhat run-down, the building is still standing, with commercial realtors seeking to refresh and lease the space.

TOP RIGHT The treatment of the upper portion of the façade gives the building its Zigzag character. Pale-orange porcelain-enameled panels with a ziggurat profile crown the double-hung windows; step-back and multiple-plane detailing enlivens the taller and shorter brick pilasters.

RIGHT Multiple-plane pilasters that extend beyond the precast-concrete parapet adorn the buff-brick building's two-storey façade, seen here in 1993. Notice the large protruding letters above the ground floor that spell out the company name, and the curved windows framing the corner entrance.

Holt Renfrew

1300 Sherbrooke Street, Montreal, Quebec
Ross & Macdonald, 1937

The luxury fashion retailer we now know as Holt Renfrew was founded in 1837, when Irish-born merchant William S. Henderson bought out his partners in a Quebec City fur shop. Henderson sold such products as fur muffs and scarves, buffalo robes and bearskins, some of which he manufactured himself. In 1862, his nephew, George Richard Renfrew, became a partner in the business, while the 1910 promotion of former company clerk John Henderson Holt to president resulted in the company's name becoming Holt, Renfrew and Company Limited.

In 1886, Queen Victoria personally purchased several of the company's furs at the Indian & Colonial Exhibition in London. As a result, it was appointed furrier to the Queen; the final such warrant being issued in 1921 by the future King Edward VIII.

To honour its centenary in 1937, Holts moved from busy St. Catherine Street West and built a new flagship store at the corner of Sherbrooke and Mountain Streets. This location was just steps away from the prestigious Ritz-Carlton Hotel; the company believed Sherbrooke would become 'Montreal's Fifth Avenue.'

This Streamlined Moderne store drew praise from a range of sources: New York industry journal *Women's Wear Daily* commented on September 7, 1937, that it was "one of the most modernly and attractively appointed retail establishments on this continent." The article went on to describe the store's merchandising strategy: "Throughout the building, stock is concealed, and the main room in each department is in the nature of a lounge."

Furs and accessories were sold on the ground floor, coats and hats on the second, and dresses on the third floor. A beauty shop and executive offices occupied the fourth floor, while factory space – and storage vaults for 15,000 coats – filled the remaining two floors.

The company's royal connection continued when, in 1947, the Canadian government commissioned Holts to design a Labrador wild milk coat as the wedding gift for Princess Elizabeth on her marriage to Prince Philip.

ABOVE Six storeys tall when first constructed, the buff-coloured Indiana limestone building with a polished Stanstead granite base exhibited many attributes of the Streamlined Moderne style. Foremost among these was the large rounded corner, complete with wraparound windows; other features included subtle speed stripes at the edges of the façade, horizontally proportioned window panes, and a flagpole at the roofline. Above the front window is a bas-relief carving of the royal shield, a nod to the company's heritage as furrier to the Queen. In 1947, a sympathetically designed, six-storey extension was added to the west; the glass-walled top floor arrived more recently.

Holt Renfrew

TOP This period photo of the second-floor coat department reveals the store's elegant interior that featured lounge-like furnishings surrounded by wood-panelled walls. Customers were waited on by salespersons who retrieved merchandise from concealed racks. Notice the rounded corners in the woodwork flanking the elevator, which is announced by graceful period lettering.

ABOVE This bas-relief of a fox is one of six carvings that flank the front façade's main window. The others depict a squirrel, ram, seal, rabbit, and, of course, a beaver.

RIGHT The building's main entrance boasts this pair of copper-and-brass doors containing low-relief depictions of five animals whose furs were sold in the store.

Hudson's Bay Company Department Store

10230 Jasper Avenue, Edmonton, Alberta
Moody & Moore, 1937–38

The oldest business institution in North America was born in 1670, when King Charles issued a royal charter that created 'The Governor and Company of Adventurers of England trading into Hudson's Bay.' Sailing aboard a wooden ship called the *Nonsuch*, the first adventurers established their headquarters at York Factory on the southwest shore of Hudson's Bay.

The company set up posts across what is now Western and Northern Canada, from which they traded furs with many groups of First Nations. One such post was Fort Edmonton, built in 1795, located near the centre of the 'York Factory Express' trading route that connected Hudson's Bay with the Pacific Ocean. Travelling by canoe or in sturdy wooden 'York boats,' traders hauled their furs and trade goods that included the company's multicoloured woolen point blankets.

When its northern territory was incorporated into the new Dominion of Canada in 1870, Hudson's Bay Company diversified its operations and began selling a range of general merchandise to the farmers who began populating Western Canada. Thanks in part to the arrival of the Canadian Pacific Railway in 1885, the company decided to establish a store in Edmonton five years later.

By 1926, the company had assembled land stretching a full block eastward on Jasper Avenue from its original location at 103rd Street, with plans to construct a large new store. Delayed by the Depression, the plans for the new two-storey Streamlined Moderne structure were unveiled in December 1937, with the building of the $1-million edifice – nearly 100 metres in length – planned in three phases to permit retail operations to continue while construction was underway. The store's first two phases were completed in time for Christmas 1938, with the remaining phase finished in September 1939.

The region's economic boom, a result of the 1947 oil strike in nearby Leduc, prompted the company to add the building's anticipated third storey in 1949. A major extension six years later doubled the store's size, making it the company's largest store in Canada.

Hudson's Bay operated the store until 1984; the building was declared a Municipal Heritage Resource in 1989. It gained new life when the University of Alberta purchased the property in 2007 and established a downtown campus that it dubbed 'Enterprise Square.'

ABOVE LEFT The block-long, Streamlined Moderne structure, seen here in 1989, featured smooth limestone walls atop a 3.6-metre-tall, black-granite base that framed the large display windows. Horizontal strips of glass block brought some natural light into the second floor; the third floor, added in 1949, contained few windows. A small step-back on the Jasper Avenue roofline complemented the protruding horizontal stone bands framing the second floor.

LEFT The chamfered corners at either end of the Jasper Avenue façade were incised with the company's coat of arms that included four beavers, a fox, and two bucks, and featured the company's motto: *Pro pelle cutem* (Skin for leather). Beneath the emblems were commemorative inscriptions, one describing the granting of the company's charter, and the other referring to the founding of Fort Edmonton. Notice the rounded edges of the main walls that are adorned with short protruding speed stripes.

Hudson's Bay Company Department Store

ABOVE This period photo shows the elegant coffee shop in the store's basement, complete with stools surrounding the U-shaped counters that bore chrome-plated napkin holders, bottles of sugar, ashtrays, and salt-and-pepper shakers. Notice the bank of milkshake makers, giant coffee urns, the bouquets of flowers, and the elegant period lettering on the rear wall.

RIGHT The building's only decorative elements were giant incised carvings above the store's entrances, depicting scenes from the company's history. This carving of a trapper is joined by five others: a farmer with a plough, the *Nonsuch* sailing vessel, a York boat, a settler on a wagon, and a First Nations buffalo hunter on horseback.

F.W. Woolworth Department Store

St. Catherine Street West at McGill College Avenue, Montreal, Quebec
Archibald & Illsley, 1937–38 (demolished 1986)

Franklin Winfield Woolworth had a lifelong passion for selling; as a young child in upstate New York, he would play 'store,' setting up merchandise to sell to his brother Charles. After attending a business college in nearby Watertown, he got a job as a stock boy, where his gift for merchandising became evident. His first foray into retailing – a five-cent store in Utica, New York – failed after only three weeks; undeterred, he headed to southern Pennsylvania and opened a new store that offered merchandise costing up to 10 cents. The business expanded rapidly, encompassing 586 'five-and-dime' stores when F.W. Woolworth Company was incorporated in 1911.

F.W. was so personally wealthy that, in 1913, he opened the world's tallest building – the $13.5-million, 60-storey, Woolworth Building in New York City – that he paid for in cash. This neo-Gothic skyscraper was clad with terracotta tiles, a material that would be widely used in Woolworth's stores in the future.

In its heyday, beyond its stores in cities across the United States and Canada, the company ran stores in the United Kingdom, Ireland, Germany, Austria, Mexico, and Cyprus; curiously, Woolworth's stores located in Australia, New Zealand, and South Africa were not related to F.W. Woolworth Company.

After passing beneath the usual striped awning, shoppers usually found a lunch counter – often in the basement – complete with swiveling stools, float machines, plenty of chrome trim, and prominent signage that announced such menu items as turkey dinners, fries, milkshakes, banana splits – and, of course, Coca-Cola.

In 1962, aiming to serve growing suburban markets without weakening its flagship downtown stores, the company launched the Woolco chain of discount department outlets. Ultimately however, Woolworth's did not survive the changes in customer buying patterns, as well as pressures from such global competitors as Sam Walton's Wal-Mart.

TOP Clad in cream-coloured terracotta, the three-storey flagship F.W. Woolworth store in downtown Montreal resembled many larger company stores in the U.S. and elsewhere. Its Zigzag styling included step-back massing, multiple planes, and simple geometric decoration on the spandrel panels. Seen here after the original store had closed but before its 1986 demolition, the solid strip of wall above the ground floor once boasted the usual gold-coloured 'F.W. Woolworth' lettering on a dark red background, complete with the diamond-shaped 'W' emblem over the corner entrance.

ABOVE This Kitchener, Ontario store – seen here in 1992 – was typical of smaller-market Woolworth's outlets. The façade's styling features Zigzag elements – the step-back roofline above the second-floor windows, each topped with a vertically fluted panel – as well as such Streamlined details as the recessed speed stripes near the parapet, and the subtle circular 'porthole' motifs between the window groupings. The branding on the canopy shows the company's updated logo. Woolworth's has since left the building, which currently houses a discount store.

Department Stores

Zeller's Department Store

1595 Barrington Street, Halifax, Nova Scotia
Grattan Dalrymple Thompson, 1938–39

For several years, Kitchener, Ontario – born Walter P. Zeller managed the Canadian operations of American retailer Schulte-United, but when the Depression hit and the company declared bankruptcy, Zeller bought back 14 of the stores that he had previously sold to them to support their expansion into Canada, and rebranded them to Zeller's. Within a year, Zeller's was operating a dozen downtown stores in southwestern Ontario, Quebec, and New Brunswick.

Zeller's was a generous employer for its time, launching a group life insurance program and group pension plans in the midst of World War II. The discount retailer's motto – "Quality goods at low prices" – struck a chord with Canadians, as the chain grew to 60 stores by its 25th anniversary in 1957.

The Zellers chain – now without the apostrophe in its name – continued to expand after being acquired by Hudson's Bay Company in 1978. But stiff competition from Wal-Mart Canada eventually caused many of its stores to be sold to Target Canada in 2011, with the final Zellers store closing in 2013.

The 1938–39 Halifax Zeller's store – built at a cost of $250,000 – was situated on a sloping, 915-square-metre corner lot that faced Barrington Street. Barrington was the cultural and commercial centre of the city, accessible by electric trolleys, where Haligonians shopped, banked, dined – and watched movies at the 1930 Capitol Theatre (designed to look like a castle; demolished in 1977 to make way for an office and retail complex).

In describing the new Zeller's store, a period journal noted that its "decorative motifs are not too profuse and lines are simple… A building of this class is an asset to any community and its owners may well feel proud of it."

After Zellers moved out of the building it housed the city's Discovery Centre on its upper floors from 1995 to early 2017. Following considerable debate, the structure – which lacked heritage designation – is being transformed into residences. The Art Deco façades on Barrington and Sackville Streets are being retained, while a curved-glass, 11-storey tower will rise from its roof.

TOP Wrapping around the two-storey main floor was a mezzanine that boasted sleek chrome handrails and a terrazzo floor. Neatly organized counters displayed the store's merchandise; clerks occupied the narrow space between the counters, ready to ring in each shopper's purchases. The toy department was in the basement, with general offices and storage space on the top floor.

ABOVE Three storeys tall with a full basement, the reinforced-concrete building was clad in smooth Wallace sandstone above a black granite base. Seen here in 2005, its Zigzag features include vertically arranged windows on the Barrington and Granville Street façades, and slight step-backs at the roofline. By contrast, a series of Streamlined stone bands above the first floor were intermittently adorned with bas-relief carvings whose subjects included geese, fish, and floral motifs. Originally, the store's front entrance was centred on the Barrington Street façade, and surrounded by display windows. A carved 'Z' appears beneath the metal grillwork on the chamfered corner, which once displayed the store's name.

Peardon Building

168 Great George Street, Charlottetown, Prince Edward Island
Edward Sterling Blanchard, 1930

Initially designed for Stanley, Shaw and Peardon – a local heating, plumbing, and hardware business founded in 1901 – this stylish 'mixed-use' building has been occupied by a range of tenants since its construction. In 1937, the city directory's listing of its occupants included the Rose Marie Hairdressing Parlor, the P.E.I. Mutual Fire Insurance Company, the fruit branch of the Dominion Department of Agriculture, the Canadian Farm Loan Board, a produce exporter – and Mrs. Florence Betts. The following year, Mrs. Betts opened Betts Fur Salon, which specialized in making capes and neckpieces from locally farmed silver foxes – a thriving industry on the island early in the century. Such capes sometimes included the fox's feet, tail, and head, a frightening sight for young children sitting behind women wearing them in church! A later city directory indicated that 10 units in the building's upper floors were used as residences. In the years since, the structure has seen many retail and commercial establishments come and go.

The red bricks that clad the Peardon Building were formed from the province's natural clay deposits; the island's sandstone bedrock, rich in iron oxide, produces its famous red soil that – together with ideal climatic conditions – accounts for the province's billion-dollar potato industry.

LEFT The symmetrical façade on the three-storey, red-brick building – seen here in 1994 – boasted a range of Zigzag-style elements, including the protruding brick piers framing pairs of double-hung windows, and the multiple-plane treatment of the central and end bays with their narrower windows. The tops of these three bays have been significantly altered; they once protruded more than a metre above the parapet and featured stone trim in a bold step-back profile. Originally, the ground floor consisted of wood-framed doors and shop windows, topped by canvas awnings.

TOP Various brickwork patterns enlivened the building's main façade. Darker brown bricks were used to create diamond 'diaper' patterns above the third floor, and to accentuate the tops of the main piers. On the wall above the second floor, the bricks were laid with vertical joints, except for the locations of the narrow piers. Notice the alternating large and small stone dentils that accent the roofline.

St. James Public Market

1125 Ontario Street East, Montreal, Quebec

Trudel & Karch, 1931

Erected to replace an 1872 structure in the same location, the 'Marché St-Jacques' opened for business on November 13, 1931. Built at a cost of $325,000 as part of a provincial and municipal job-creation program (along with two other markets), the market's elevated ground floor contained 10 stalls – from which local farmers and other merchants sold their fresh fish, meats, and garden produce – together with public washrooms and the manager's office. The building's upper floor, reached by three staircases, housed an auditorium space that featured a raised stage and dressing rooms. Above the auditorium was a mezzanine level containing cloakroom space and a small balcony. The market's manager lived in a three-bedroom apartment split between the auditorium level and the mezzanine.

A particularly noteworthy event took place at the market on February 11, 1942, two months prior to Liberal Prime Minister Mackenzie King's national plebiscite on conscription for World War II. An anti-conscription rally – organized by the *Ligue pour la defense du Canada* that was established by future Montreal mayor Jean Drapeau – filled the building's auditorium and attracted thousands more outside, who listened to the speeches via a rented $300 sound system. Despite the more measured remarks of French-Canadian nationalist Henri Bourassa – who had staunchly opposed federal conscription policies since the Boer War – angry nationalist supporters marched through the city streets following the rally, injuring eight policemen and landing 18 protesters in jail. The plebiscite ultimately attracted nearly two-thirds support across Canada, but 72 percent opposition in Quebec.

The city continued to own St. James Market – including using its upper floor as office space – until 2006, when it was sold to a developer. The ground floor now houses a dozen boutique food shops, while the upper level is being converted to two-level condominiums.

ABOVE Seen here before its brick façade was refreshed, the Zigzag-style building's symmetrical, multiple-plane front façade terminated in a step-back, copper-roofed tower that made the building stand out from its low-rise Centre-Sud neighbours. Double-hung windows with vertical panes, arranged in recessed vertical strips, added to the building's perceived height. The canopy-covered, open-air market, backed by separate shops, was located on the left side of the building in this photo.

ABOVE LEFT Flanking the main entrance are semi-circular French balconies decorated with geometric patterns and depictions of the market's produce, in this case, pineapples. The bas-relief panel at the rear shows a corn stalk.

ABOVE This period view of a typical stall shows its refrigerated room at the rear, plus its white enamel and stainless steel display case facing the main shopping corridor. A small office containing a sink is concealed behind the column. The steps down to the street level continued down to the basement that contained refrigerated cellars for each stall. Notice the stepped profile of the beams above the stalls and corridor, the multiple, vertically proportioned glass panes in the doors, and the geometric frosted-glass chandelier.

RIGHT The decoration atop the ground floor's chamfered corner includes cast-concrete bas-relief carvings of squid and fish. Decorations elsewhere included mollusks, bees, and flowers.

McLennan, McFeely and Prior Building

811 Columbia Street, New Westminster, British Columbia
McCarter & Nairne, 1938–39

Thanks to its strategic position on the north shore of the mighty Fraser River, its distance from the American border, and its views of the surrounding mountains, the Columbia Detachment of Britain's Royal Engineers chose today's New Westminster, in 1858, as the capital of its new mainland Colony of British Columbia. Given its name by Queen Victoria, 'The Royal City' – incorporated in 1860 – relinquished its capital status eight years later, when that colony merged with the Colony of Vancouver Island, and Victoria was named the capital of the future province of British Columbia.

New Westminster's economic fortunes grew during that period's gold rushes, and it remained an important port, lumber producer, and commercial centre serving the Fraser River Valley. The city's Columbia Street, running parallel to the Fraser River, attracted major department stores and cinemas in the early decades of the twentieth century.

In 1885, Pictou, Nova Scotia – born Robert Purves McLennan partnered with Lindsay, Ontario – born Edward John McFeely to establish McLennan, McFeely and Company Limited, based in Victoria. Soon moving to Vancouver, the firm's business was importing and distributing hardware and building supplies. It eventually operated a number of outlets across the province, all served from its giant warehouse in Vancouver's Gastown district. McLennan and McFeely were both established members of the city's business community, with McFeely focusing on the Vancouver operations. In the late 1920s, E.G. Prior joined the company as a third partner.

Designed by architects McCarter & Nairne of Marine Buiding fame (see page 8), and constructed on a large corner lot on the north side of Columbia Street, the 1939 Streamlined Moderne store signalled a renewed sense of prosperity after the challenging Depression years. A 1951 catalogue reveals that the business, widely known as Mc. & Mc., had expanded its retail product line to include sporting goods. During the 1960s, major British industrial supplier Acklands purchased the company; the building later housed a Salvation Army Thrift Store.

Listed on the Community Heritage Register in 2004, the building's Columbia Street façade is all that now remains, having been incorporated into the newly constructed 'Shops at New West' project that is attached to the upgraded New Westminster SkyTrain light rapid transit station.

ABOVE Rounded corners softened the appearance of this three-storey Streamlined Moderne structure, seen here in 1940. Octagonal interior concrete columns with spread capitals supported its flat roof; the exterior finish was smoothly poured concrete, showing faint traces of the horizontal and vertical formwork. The principal façade facing Columbia Street, bearing the company full name, steps-up slightly above the roofline; the third floor features a near-continuous ribbon of horizontally proportioned windowpanes that include large circular panes at opposite ends. Wrapping across the second-floor corner wall was the company's popular name, Mc. & Mc. A giant neon-illuminated clock, complete with a swinging pendulum, projected out from the main façade. Notice the series of refrigerators displayed in the ground-floor corner window.

Robbins Drug Store

17 Charlotte Street, Saint John, New Brunswick
Allward & Gillies, 1939 (demolished)

Opened just as World War II was beginning, Robbins Drug Store – with its soda bar and lunch counter – did a thriving business serving navy men and members of the Canadian Merchant Navy who helped to defend the port of Saint John throughout the war.

A 1942 postcard trumpeted the store's "Magic 'Electric Eye' doors [which] say 'Welcome' is the word at Robbins – Eastern Canada's most modern Drug Store." Inside, the long lunch counter on the right side faced freestanding and wall-mounted display cases that sold all manner of name-brand cosmetics, soaps, and confectionery. The store's yellow-and-red Eddy Match Company paper matchbooks were emblazoned with a pair of robins, and announced that the air-conditioned shop was 'So handy on Charlotte Street.'

Some time after the departure of its original owners, the store was owned and operated by Freda and Lee April – both 1960 graduates from Dalhousie University's School of Pharmacy – who sold the business to Shoppers Drug Mart in 1971. Sadly, this unique building was demolished some years later.

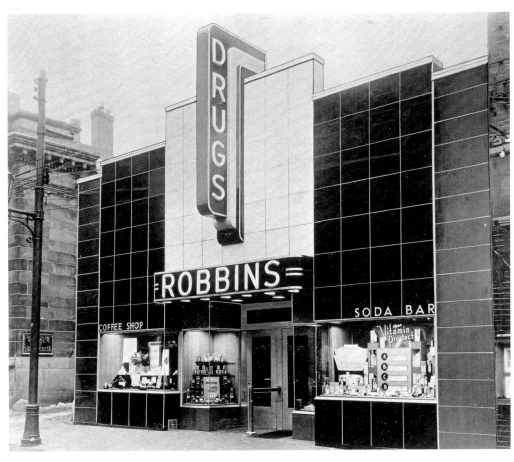

ABOVE Perfume bottles lined the shelves behind the cosmetics counter, while Christmas-themed chocolates were displayed next to a selection of pipes, cigars, and cans of tobacco. To the left of the doll display at the rear was the entrance to the dispensary, 'truss department,' and office. Notice the circular ceiling lights and the chrome torchères located inside the display cases.

RIGHT A row of chrome-and-leather stools faced the shelves of sparkling float glasses – "Malted Milk Shakes: 15¢" – that flanked the cooking zone topped by a rounded-corner fan hood. Through the arch at the rear were the restrooms and phones.

TOP The Streamlined Moderne façade of Robbins Drug Store, seen here in 1950, set it dramatically apart from neighbouring buildings. The symmetrical storefront – dominated by a theatre-style projecting vertical marquee – was clad in light and dark colours of Vitrolite panels. Its slightly protruding entrance canopy, bearing the store's name framed by speed stripes, featured recessed lights to illuminate the corner display windows – one promoting 50¢ cough syrup – that flanked the chrome front doors.

Photo credits: Library and Archives Canada, Allward & Gillies Collection. Top: 1979-122 2000753319; Above: E007913790; Right: 186376.

R.J. O'Brien General Store

Harbour Road, Cape Broyle, Newfoundland
Ronald J. O'Brien (builder), 1946

Located on 'the Irish Loop' on Newfoundland's Avalon Peninsula, 64 kilometres south of St. John's along Route 10, the fishing village of Cape Broyle dates back to the 1780s. Its name comes from the Portuguese term *brolle* (to roar), a reference to the whitewater formed when waves pounded a sunken rock ledge jutting out into the ocean.

This unique general store is located on Harbour Road (also known as Lower Road); prior to the construction of a fish-processing plant, it had a clear southern view of the bay facing the Atlantic Ocean. The owner of the General Store, Ronald (R.J.) O'Brien constructed it himself, with the assistance of two carpenters named Jim Jones and Little Mickey O'Brien. Like the store's exterior, its interior was composed of wood, with planks on the floor and a tongue-and-groove wooden ceiling; the door into the office was curved in keeping with the exterior.

An unusual story explains the existence of the west-facing round corner. In its early days, each time Mr. O'Brien was driving his carriage or sleigh westward past the building and turned right around the sharp bend in the road to reach his home just up the hill, his horses kept hitting the squared corner of the store. He solved the problem by rounding the corner, repeating the curve on the east-facing corner.

At present, the Registered Heritage Structure houses a sea kayak outfitting company that has carefully preserved its unique character.

ABOVE Two rounded corners made of wooden shingles lent a sense of streamlining to this one-storey, shed-roofed building that was otherwise clad in narrow clapboard. The rounded corners framing the double-door main entrance were made of concrete, and adorned with a series of three vertical speed stripes. A narrow plank loading-door was located on the rounded east corner; large wooden shutters protected the plate-glass shop windows from storms coming off the ocean. Above the door is the original sign, reading 'R.J. O'Brien General Dealer.'

Cabot Building

221 Duckworth Street, St. John's, Newfoundland
William J. Ryan, 1947

In the decades prior to Newfoundland's entry into Confederation in 1949, the practice of architecture was quite informal, with architects learning their trade by apprenticing with those already working in the field. The fact they sometimes served as the contractor on their own projects – in this case, the architect was the building's structural engineer as well as its contractor – meant it was easier for them to have their designs constructed precisely as planned. However, since modern materials enjoyed by architects in the rest of Canada were not available, island practitioners were forced to rely on simpler construction techniques. Being less constrained by mainstream design traditions, Newfoundland architects produced some unique and eclectic buildings. The Cabot Building from 1947 – likely named in honour of the British-commissioned explorer who discovered the island – was one such novel structure.

In the building's early days, it housed William Ryan's architectural practice; later occupants included a law firm, trust company, radio station, and a bookstore. Over the years, the building's interior deteriorated, necessitating structural repairs and modernization to make it comply with building codes.

In 2009, the building received the Newfoundland & Labrador Historic Trust's Southcott Award in the Building Restoration / Preservation category. The award recognized the retention of the façade's Art Deco details, combined with the addition of new horizontally proportioned windows, a bold new entrance feature, and pastel colours. It's little wonder that the revitalized structure is now called the South Beach Building.

TOP Seen here in 1994, the front entrance of the building is graced with several Deco-era details. Among these are the subtle grooves in the protruding piers flanking the entrance, the multilayered, projecting rectangles above the first floor, and the twin panels of incised vertical fluting at the roofline. An interesting transposition of numerals exists at the centre of the parapet: 1497 marking Cabot's arrival on the shores of the island, and 1947 announcing the building's date of construction.

LEFT The two-storey structure, built without a setback from the sidewalk, was constructed of poured-in-place concrete – a favourite material of its architect. Its symmetrical façade incorporated a range of period motifs, including the protruding horizontal band atop the second floor, the uninterrupted piers at the corners, and the increased height of the parapet above the central bay.

Showrooms and Exhibition Buildings

Automotive Building

105 Princes' Boulevard, Toronto, Ontario
Douglas Edwin Kertland, 1929

Although a steam-powered 'horseless carriage' had been invented back in 1867 by Henry Seth Taylor of Stanstead, Quebec, the Canadian automobile industry began in earnest in 1904 when Gordon McGregor – whose father was a wagon builder – persuaded Henry Ford to let him manufacture and sell Ford automobiles in Canada. In its first year, Ford Motor Company of Canada – located in Walkerville, a downtown district in today's Windsor, Ontario – built 117 cars; its output climbed to more than 51,000 units by 1922. Also in Windsor, Chrysler set up shop in the early 1920s.

Meanwhile, Robert Samuel (Sam) McLaughlin – born just north of Oshawa, Ontario – started the McLaughlin Motor Car Company in 1907, using American-made Buick engines to produce the McLaughlin-Buick Model F. The 1918 merger of McLaughlin's company with the Chevrolet Motor Company of Canada created General Motors of Canada Limited.

In addition to supplying vehicles for the country's war effort, car manufacturing in Canada took off in the early decades of the twentieth century due to stiff tariff barriers on imported vehicles, and because the country – as part of the British Empire – could export cars to other Empire countries more cheaply than could American firms.

From their earliest days, automobiles captured the attention of Canadians. Cars were first displayed at the Canadian National Exhibition in Toronto in 1897; their growing popularity led to the formation of the National Motor Show in 1916. When the CNE's Transportation Building became too crowded, it was decided, in 1928, that a new purpose-built structure was required to hold the twice-annual show.

Thirty submissions were made to the 'Competition for an Automotive Building' that was announced on October 31, with submissions due just a month later. The winner, Toronto architect Douglas Kertland, was obliged to subtract his $2,500 first prize from the 6 percent commission earned for designing the building. The project was characterized in a period journal as a 'rush job'; its construction drawings needed to be prepared in less than four weeks. The construction contract was awarded March 26, 1929; remarkably, the million-dollar structure was essentially completed by August 23rd – opening day of that year's Exhibition.

In describing the new building, the same journal made two points about its design. "First is the general impression one gathers of classical dignity and almost Grecian restraint; the other, paradoxically enough, is the effect of modernity." In today's vocabulary, the building is an excellent example of the Stripped Classical style.

Rectangular in plan, the building provided over 11,000 square metres of skylit display space for automobiles, trucks, and buses on the ground floor; the surrounding mezzanine level showcased accessories, and included a kitchen, dining room, and meeting room. Visitors could use the north-facing main entrance, or a matching southern entrance that overlooked a landscaped area, Lake Shore Boulevard West, and Lake Ontario beyond.

The building was used for other purposes beyond the Motor Show; in September 1931 for instance, it hosted the American Hospital Association Convention. During World War II, the Automotive Building served as a naval recruitment facility, but was actively used for auto shows for the following five decades.

The building was brought back to life in 2009 with the completion of a major renovation that restored the exterior façade and entrance halls, but transformed the interior into a state-of-the-art convention and meeting facility. The restoration / adaptation earned an Award of Merit in the William Greer Architectural Conservation and Craftsmanship category at the 2010 Heritage Toronto Awards.

ABOVE The two-storey Automotive Building – seen here in September 1940 – is more than 140 metres wide by 90 metres deep, and clad in artificial stone meant to resemble Indiana limestone. While its symmetrical massing and grand proportions harken back to an earlier age, its simplified façades and decorative motifs place it firmly in the Stripped Classical design tradition. The prominent 'Motor Show' signage appeared at all four corners of the structure.

City of Toronto Archives, Fonds 1548, Series 393, Item 25129F.

ABOVE In this view of the main (north-facing) entrance, all the traditional architectural elements – the shallow pediment, triple rounded arches, and corner pilasters – have been gracefully simplified and flattened. Notice the stylized floral motifs atop the pilasters, and the traditional Roman spelling of the word 'AVTOMOTIVE' on the unadorned architrave.

Automotive Building

ABOVE LEFT Matching staircases to the mezzanine level flank the foyer that opens into the renovated building's pre-function space. The coffered ceiling treatment and black-and-white square terrazzo flooring match the original design.

Small bas-reliefs of the faces of Canadian animals adorn the wall above the inner doors; this may reflect the fact that Douglas Kertland once worked in the office of John M. Lyle, the 'champion' of Canadian-themed ornamentation.

ABOVE RIGHT The two-storey, classically inspired portico at the north entry creates a grand arrival experience. The three sets of doors are topped by windows with vertical panes that bring daylight into the mezzanine level. Notice the multiple planes framing the windows, and the metal grilles that create the impression of French balconies. The chandeliers are modern replicas of the original fixtures.

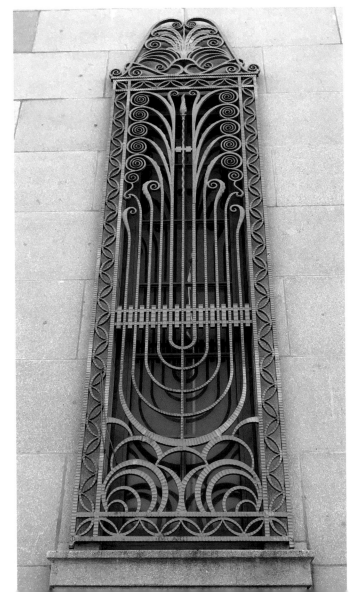

LEFT Cast-iron grilles, made to appear like bronze, protect the slender windows at various locations on the façades. Their decorative features include delicate swirls capping the central bars, concentric circles at the base, and the pyramidal floral detail that crowns the grille. Similar Zigzag-era floral motifs adorn the spandrel panels on the main stretches of wall.

TOP LEFT This period view of the south mezzanine level reveals the simple fluting of the pilasters, and the wonderful frosted-glass geometric chandeliers. The ceiling beams are decorated with the winged wheel motif – a popular symbol for transportation that still adorns the jerseys of the hockey team in 'Motor City': the Detroit Red Wings.

ABOVE Bathed in natural light from the end-to-end skylights, the ground-floor showroom – seen here in 1936 – displays the latest and greatest automobiles, some on elevated streamlined turntables and others on carpets. Zigzag-style motifs adorn the edges of the mezzanine level. The fact that the Union Jack flag hangs alongside the Canadian Red Ensign reflects Toronto's continuing close connection with Britain. The Hupmobile vehicle in the lower-left corner of the photo would cease production three years later.

Horse Palace

15 Nova Scotia Avenue, Toronto, Ontario
J.J. Woolnough, 1931

Following World War I, a group of farmers established the Agricultural Winter Fair Association of Canada as a forum for judging domestic animals. After the Coliseum Building on the Toronto Exhibition Grounds first hosted the Royal Agricultural Winter Fair in 1922, it became evident that more stable space was needed to accommodate horses associated with that annual event.

The Horse Palace – referred to as the 'Horse Building' by its architect and as the 'Fair Stables' or 'Exhibition Stables' in *Toronto Star* headlines of the day – was constructed in five months at a cost of $900,000. It opened on August 15, 1931, just in time for that summer's Canadian National Exhibition and 'The Royal' later that autumn.

Clad in buff-brick and stone, the steel-frame Horse Palace building contained 30,000 square metres of space. It housed 1,200 stalls of varying sizes, spread over two floors, that were linked by several ramps with cleated planking. An exercise wing measuring 56 by 18 metres and topped by a glass cathedral ceiling occupied the centre of the building. Along the west side were public washrooms and a horse barber shop; to the east were hospital stalls, veterinary offices, a blacksmith shop, and covered passages leading to the Coliseum. A period journal noted that, beyond horses, the upper floor housed fox exhibits, plus dressing rooms and living space for the horses' support staff. A freight elevator hoisted straw and horse feed to storage space on the third floor.

During World War II, the Horse Palace served as a barracks for Canadian soldiers yet to be sent overseas, as well as a demobilization centre after the war.

Since it first opened, the Horse Palace has housed the Toronto Police Mounted Division; today, it also contains a city Animal Services branch and a private riding academy.

Although the design of the Horse Palace is generally credited to City of Toronto architect John James Woolnough, Deputy City Architect Kenneth S. Gillies assisted with the design and preparation of drawings, together with staff architect Stanley T.J. Fryer.

ABOVE The frieze stretching across the top of the southwest-facing portico features a low-relief carving of a prancing horse; the three panels above the entrance contain twin roundel, of horse heads – each bracketed by three speed stripes – that frame the central panel with 'Horses' incised in 1930s lettering. Crisp horizontal bands cap the smooth octagonal columns.

RIGHT The octagonal shape of the cupola is carried through into the lamp standards. Notice the use of multiple planes on the support brackets, as well as on the bases of the lights themselves.

ABOVE This southwest view of the buff-brick Horse Palace shows the predominantly horizontal emphasis of the windows and Queenston stone trim. The southernmost of the two entrance porticos framing the staircase tower is visible at the left.

Horse Palace

ABOVE Even the entrance to the women's washroom reflects the building's equine theming; the carved panel above the door features the rear-ends of two horses, complete with streamlined tails.

RIGHT Four multi-layer, carved horse-head profiles mark the base of the domed octagonal cupola that crowns the stair tower on the west façade. The tower's verticality is offset by the three brick speed stripes at the top of the wall. Notice the multiple-plane zigzags and half-discs inside the top of the narrow, two-storey rounded arch.

World Grain Show Building

Exhibition Grounds, Regina, Saskatchewan
Storey & Van Egmond, 1931–32 (destroyed by fire 1955 & 2009)

Saskatchewan's reputation as the 'bread basket of the world' was confirmed by its hosting of the World Grain Exhibition and Conference in Regina during the summer of 1933. Announced in 1928 – when times were good for agriculture in the province – the two-week event was intended to take place during the city's 50th anniversary in 1932, but was ultimately postponed for a year. The exhibition's slogan was 'Show what you grow, share what you know.'

The show's grain competition involved prizes totalling $200,000 – the "Greatest Cash Prize List Ever Offered," its organizers claimed – and was promoted with 25,000 posters and 75,000 brochures. By 1930, the list of countries that would attend included the U.S., the United Kingdom, and France, as well as such faraway lands as the Philippine Islands, Chile, and Siam.

Housed in the new $200,000 World Grain Show Building, the event featured scientific and academic papers – whose topics included 'The Present World Wheat Situation' and 'Causes of Agricultural Depression' – that were delivered by international agricultural researchers. Meanwhile, visitors to the adjacent annual Regina Fair enjoyed the midway, performances of the opera *Aida*, as well as shows by the Japanese Aerial Performers and The Nighthawks radio entertainers. Visitors stayed at local hotels, as well as at a 20-hectare tent city accommodating 3,000 people. The final tally indicated that over 210,000 people attended the conference and exhibition, which has sadly been largely forgotten.

The Grain Show Building continued to host events after the 1933 Exhibition, but fire destroyed its centre and west wings in 1955 and later consumed its neglected east wing in 2009.

TOP The Zigzag styling of the building's east wing entrance, seen here in 1994, includes the step-back profile and multiple-plane treatment of its piers, along with the colourful chevrons and geometric patterns on its white stucco surface.

RIGHT This architectural rendering hardly captures the immense scale of the U-shaped, one-storey exhibit hall that stretched more than 250 metres in length, with matching 90-metre wings. In total, the structure housed over three kilometres of exhibit space. The façades boasted coats-of-arms of the more than 50 participating nations, each topped with the country's flag.

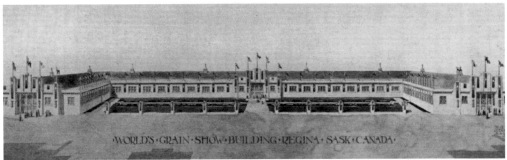

International Harvester Building

550 Wellington Street West, Toronto, Ontario

Neil A. Armstrong, 1940

Patented in 1834, the horse-drawn reaper developed by the McCormick Harvesting Machine Company of Chicago soon became a popular implement on American farms. A few years after the company's founder passed away in 1885, McCormick joined with four other firms to establish the International Harvester Company, with J.P. Morgan arranging the financing. Soon after, the new company purchased a plough manufacturer; its line of Farmall tractors began production in the 1920s. In 1939, American industrial designer Raymond Loewy created International Harvester's 'letter series' of general purpose tractors that continued to sell well for two decades, despite strong competition from John Deere, Ford, and other manufacturers.

After operating out of a showroom space on Bay Street near the Ontario Legislature Building in Toronto, the International Harvester Company of Canada Limited decided to construct a new sales and service facility for its line of trucks. Situated at the northeast corner of Bathurst and Wellington Streets, the new 4,400-square-metre building stretched 45 metres north along Bathurst and more than double that length eastward along Wellington. The front of the building housed the showroom; the mostly open space to the rear – fully spanned by giant steel trusses – contained service bays, a parts department, and warehouse space, as well as a rest room complete with showers for use by truck drivers awaiting repairs. Construction of the $185,000 structure began on October 1939 and was completed six months later.

On opening day, the company's sales director remarked that "we have incorporated in this modern structure all of the facilities and equipment that will provide prompt and efficient service for our customers...[we are proud] that it is contributing effectively to the healthy progress of the whole Dominion."

After International Harvester departed, an auto shop named Crangle's Collision occupied the building. The valuable real estate was eventually sold, and a new hotel arose in its place. The hotel's upscale diner operates within the reconstructed front façade of the original showroom.

TOP Seen here a few months after its opening, the mostly one-storey, flat-roofed, Streamlined Moderne building featured rounded corners, horizontally proportioned panes of glass on the second floor, and a dazzling main entrance sheathed in wine-coloured Carrara glass. The walls of the main-floor showroom were primarily plate glass, with awning-type windows above.

ABOVE The building's solid curved corner is visible in this period photo of the second-floor interior. Streamlined metal chandeliers and aluminum-frame windows – concealed by the closed metal blinds – illuminated the mostly open-plan, air-conditioned office that housed the company's managers, as well as the sales promotion, accounting, and stenographic departments.

City of Toronto Archives, Series 371, Sub-Series 33, Item 715.

LEFT This period photo reveals the wide range of trucks, tractors, and engines on display in the naturally lit, 510-square-metre showroom. Its solid walls were faced with ivory-coloured glazed tiles, while the floor was surfaced in a sturdy green terrazzo.

TOP LEFT The building's original cladding – buff-coloured, precast stone panels and pressed red brick – is visible in this 1993 photo of the front façade. Although a row of stone veneer above the window was missing and the painted window mullions were peeling, the original flagpole with its splendid curved base was still intact.

BOTTOM LEFT A reconstructed version of the heritage-listed building's front façade is what remains of the original structure.

Restaurants

Round Room Restaurant

7th Floor, Eaton's College Street Store, 444 Yonge Street, Toronto, Ontario
Jacques Carlu (architect), 1929–30; restored 2001–03

Born in humble circumstances in the small town of Omemee, Ontario, Flora McCrea's life as a nurse at a private hospital was forever changed when, at the tender age of 21, she married John Craig (Jack) Eaton, the son and heir to the fortune of department store legend Timothy Eaton. When Jack was knighted in 1915 for his contribution to the war effort, Flora became Lady Eaton, a title she retained until her death in 1970.

After Jack's premature death from pneumonia in 1922, Lady Eaton assumed a greater role in the retail empire's business affairs, including taking on the task of improving the store's restaurants. The first of her restaurants to open, in 1924, was 'The Georgian Room,' located on the ninth floor of the main (Queen Street) store. As new Eaton's stores were opened during the 1920s elsewhere across Canada, each one incorporated a restaurant of one form or another.

Lady Eaton regularly journeyed to Europe on business, particularly enjoying life aboard the new luxury ocean liners. So, when the new upscale Eaton's store at Yonge and College Streets (see page 173) was being built, she drew upon her experiences of transatlantic crossings in planning how best to create a series of public spaces on the building's top floor that would allow Torontonians to dine, lounge, and be entertained in elegant surroundings. To implement her vision, Lady Eaton retained Paris-born architect Jacques Carlu, whose talents she was familiar with from his designs for the *Île de France* liner.

In creating the Seventh Floor – which also housed Eaton Auditorium (see page 262), two two smaller dining rooms (The Clipper Rooms) and other spaces – Carlu oversaw every aspect of the design, including the restaurant's furniture, light fixtures, glassware, and china. At his request, the waitresses' uniforms were required to be black – to complement the room's Moderne décor. The curved walls between the restaurant's alcoves were covered with murals by Carlu's wife, Natacha; he wrote in a prestigious journal that the four painted murals "depict life in the village, the forest, the fields, and by the sea."

A promotional booklet published by Eaton's described the Round Room as "a distinguished expression of the aptness, dignity and charm of contemporary architecture and decoration," and that its details "reveal the spirit of to-day in the practical and the aesthetic." It is believed that the space was the inspiration for the Rainbow Room at New York's Rockefeller Center.

Besides serving as a restaurant, the Round Room hosted Canadian Women's Club events, men's coffee clubs, plus special presentations, flower shows, fashion shows, and debutante balls.

During the 1970s, the Round Room was unsympathetically redecorated while the new Eaton Centre was being constructed; it was shuttered in 1976. The new owners of the Eaton's College Street building sought to convert the Seventh Floor to additional office space. A campaign to protect these spaces, mounted by historic preservationists and a grassroots group called Friends of the Eaton Auditorium, ultimately resulted in a 1986 Supreme Court decision that prevented their demolition. Three years earlier, The Round Room, Eaton Auditorium, and the foyer connecting them had been recognized as National Historic Sites.

Despite this legal protection, the empty and deteriorating spaces remained closed. In 2001, Toronto entrepreneurs Jeffry Roick and Mark Robert saw the opportunity to bring Lady Eaton's vision back to life. After two years of painstaking work, the historically accurate yet technologically updated Seventh Floor reopened on May 1, 2003, as a premier event space known, rather appropriately, as The Carlu.

ABOVE The Round Room was described by the architect as a 'large coffee shop' that consisted of a domed circular room within a square. The ceiling's three-tier, glass-disc ceiling fixture was made from Lalique glass, as was the floor's circular fountain. The chairs were made of black satinwood, upholstered in a beige-coloured imitation leather called Fabrikoid. White-enamelled terracotta statuettes of peasant figures, created by French sculptor Denis Gélin, occupied the eight slender backlit niches between the four corner alcoves. Notice the sophisticated geometric pattern of the muntin bars in the frosted-glass windows.

Restaurants

LEFT The room's original colour scheme of soft lemon for the walls and ceiling – together with the Lalique fountain – have been preserved in the restored multi-functional space that still goes by the name Round Room. The murals have been fully restored, while the chandelier has been faithfully reproduced. Sections of new permanent seating have been installed in the two slightly elevated interior alcoves; a bar occupies one of the outer alcoves.

Round Room Restaurant

ABOVE This section of the Natacha Carlu painted murals depicts a formally dressed couple riding horses in the countryside.

RIGHT Designed by René Lalique and fabricated with black and frosted glass, the central fountain was connected to the room's artificial illumination to create dynamic lighting effects. It is seen here after the addition of a protective metal ring.

Eaton's Ninth Floor Restaurant

9th Floor, Eaton's Department Store, 677 St. Catharine Street West, Montreal, Quebec

Jacques Carlu, 1930–31

For almost 70 years, Eaton's Ninth Floor Restaurant – more affectionately known as *Le 9e* – played a unique role in the lives of Montrealers. It was, for instance, where women would come for lunch or afternoon tea after shopping, and where Eaton's loyal clientele would gather to socialize. The restaurant's staff and guests were the subject of a 1998 National Film Board of Canada documentary, *Les Dames du 9e (The Ladies of the 9th)*. Unfortunately, this cherished cultural experience came to an end on October 14, 1999, when the restaurant was closed – permanently – after the department store chain went into bankruptcy.

The Ninth Floor came into existence when Eaton's realized that it needed more selling space beyond its existing six-storey building located on St. Catherine Street West – the city's premier shopping thoroughfare. Consequently, construction began in 1930 on three additional floors designed by Ross & Macdonald, the top floor of which was to house a restaurant. Just as she had with the Seventh Floor of Eaton's College Street in Toronto (previous story), Lady Eaton hired architect Jacques Carlu to create a distinctive space that was inspired by the interiors of her favourite ocean liner: the 1927 *S.S. Île de France*.

The dimensions of the room – 23 metres in width by 40 metres in length – do not fully capture the Art Deco restaurant's spacious feeling. The entrance was centred on one of the long walls, so guests entered at a right angle to the room's main axis, which ran parallel to St. Catherine Street. This central axis was defined in part by large clerestory windows that admitted both daylight and artificial light. Consisting of three Streamlined bands of opal glass, curved at either end, these windows reached nearly to the room's ceiling, over 10 metres above the floor. Further delineating this axis were two rows of marble columns that separated the lower-height side dining areas from the taller central volume; the lintels between these columns were adorned with bas-reliefs – sculpted by Denis Gélin – celebrating the art of eating and drinking. Situated in a slight recess at each end of the grand space were tall murals painted by Carlu's wife, Natacha.

Two steps up from the main floor level were U-shaped floors at either end, separated from the main space by horizontally

proportioned Monel metal railings. These raised sections could be easily transformed into stages for fashion shows, with hidden spotlights already built-in. Another sign of the times were the built-in speakers, carefully concealed by metal grilles, for playing music or for use during presentations; when *Le 9e* opened on January 25, 1931, guests at lunch and afternoon tea were treated to the sounds of a live orchestra. Thanks in part to its impeccable service – delivered by waitresses dressed in pink-and-grey uniforms – there was always a lineup to get a table. In total, the restaurant could seat up to 750 guests.

After the restaurant's closure, Heritage Montreal successfully persuaded Quebec's Ministry of Culture and Communications, in 2000, to bestow official heritage status upon the Ninth Floor, thereby prohibiting any modifications or demolition of the interior or its contents. The space was also named a building of exceptional heritage value by the municipality. However, the building's owners have sealed off the Ninth Floor, preventing anyone from viewing the space – which is silently deteriorating with the passage of time.

ABOVE Fourteen elevators brought restaurant guests directly to the Ninth Floor. Furnished with Moderne couches and armchairs in shades of grey, black, and pink, the foyer occasionally served as a lounge area or tea room. Opposite the satin-finished, Monel metal doors that led into the restaurant was a series of windows with views of the St. Lawrence River in the distance. Behind its curved alcove lay the restaurant's two private dining rooms. Square and circular shop windows lined the marble corridors from the elevators to the foyer.

Eaton's Ninth Floor Restaurant

ABOVE LEFT Completed in 1960, this late Streamlined Moderne style addition extended the store all the way north to De Maisonneuve Boulevard.

ABOVE The resemblance of *Le 9e* to the *Île de France*'s first-class dining room – also designed by Jacques Carlu – is clear in this period photo. Although the tall murals and twin rows of squared, pink-and-grey marble columns create a sense of verticality, the symmetrical space's predominant styling is Streamlined Moderne. The horizontal emphasis of the clerestory windows is echoed in the subtle stripes of the beige-and-pink fabric walls. The floor consisted of seven shades of Ruboleum – a rubberized linoleum tile that was *de rigeur* in this era.

LEFT The more tranquil scene in this mural depicts one woman cradling a gazelle while others lounge or gaze at a cherub. Its title is 'The Pleasures of Peace.' Some commentators contend that the murals were deliberately intended to appeal to the restaurant's primarily female clientele.

LEFT Although the fabric walls have been replaced, the essential character of the room is evident in this 1990s photo. Giant vases, lit from within and standing on square marble bases, flanked the black marble steps that led to the raised platform at either end of the room. The bold colouration of the linoleum tile floor is clearly visible. Containing scenes of women on horseback, this Natacha Carlu mural was described in a company publicity piece as depicting 'The Pleasures of the Chase' in an 'Amazonian Arcadia.'

Eaton's Ninth Floor Restaurant

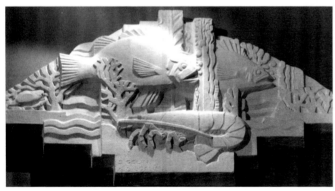

ABOVE LEFT Signed by D. Gélin & A. Bottiau, this cast-plaster bas-relief is one of 14 such works – depicting different foods and their serving vessels – that adorned the lintels above the main floor.

ABOVE Situated along the exterior wall of the restaurant were two private dining rooms – the Gold Room and the Silver Room – that each seated 40 guests who could look out a large window opposite the entrance to enjoy views of the city skyline. Artificial illumination was plentiful: lamps concealed within Monel-metal valences cast light upon the recessed ceiling; the room's corners were lit by square opal-glass pillars; and the entrance to the room was highlighted by a horizontal expanse of opal glass subdivided by vertical Monel fins. The striped curtain could be drawn to separate the room from the main dining area.

ABOVE RIGHT Deco styling extended into the smallest details; this serving stand in the main dining room combines step-back massing with rounded corners. Notice the sensational Monel metal grille with horizontal and vertical fins protruding from the marble-panelled wall.

Alexandra Hotel Tavern

30 Railway Avenue West, Drumheller, Alberta
Builder unknown, 1938

Best known today as the home of the Royal Tyrrell Museum of Palaeontology – arising from Canadian geologist Joseph Tyrrell's discovery of dinosaur bones in 1884 – the community of Drumheller's original claim to fame was its enormous coal deposits. While the local Blackfoot and Cree First Nations were well aware of the seams of combustible black rock that lined the banks of the Red Deer Valley River, it was not until 1910 that Colonel Samuel Drumheller – after selling a parcel of land to the Canadian Pacific Railway – established his own coal mine. Once the CPR began rolling through the tiny community and additional mines were opened, the economy of this badlands town took off. Drumheller's sub-bituminous coal was easier to mine since it was located in flat-lying seams and released lower amounts of dangerous methane gas. And, it was ideal as a fuel for heating, cooking, and powering electrical generators.

Not surprisingly, men from Eastern Europe, Britain, and Nova Scotia arrived in droves to work in the mines. Between 1916 and 1931, the town's population climbed from just over 300 to nearly 3,000 – almost a tenfold increase.

Some of these mine workers lived on the upper two floors of the three-storey Alexandra Hotel that was constructed on the town's main street in the mid-1930s. A 1937 fire that damaged part of the hotel also destroyed the adjoining 'Log Cabin' tavern. The next year, the popular tavern was rebuilt, this time in a striking Streamlined Moderne style.

At the industry's peak in the late 1930s, two dozen trains loaded with coal rumbled out of town each day. But the 1947 discovery of oil at Leduc, 260 kilometres north, led to natural gas becoming Western Canada's preferred heating fuel – and spelled the end of Drumheller's legendary coal boom.

TOP This view from a period postcard shows the all-white tavern that was connected to the Alexandra Hotel. Notice the band of speed stripes stretching across the main façade, and the elongated windows with chamfered corners. The word 'Drinks' appeared on the taller cylindrical corner entrance with its prominent rounded canopy.

RIGHT Although the side door and windows have been altered and its colour has changed, the building's fundamental form remains intact, as seen in this 2014 photo. Notice how the principal façade's roofline steps up twice before reaching the rounded entrance; the curved theme is continued at the top of the solid vertical fins that flank the door.

Bens De Luxe Delicatessen

900 De Maisonneuve Boulevard West, Montreal, Quebec
Charles Davis Goodman, 1950 (demolished 2008)

For celebrities – musicians such as Leonard Cohen, Michael Jackson, or Céline Dion; politicians like Pierre Trudeau, René Lévesque, or Jean Charest; or TV personalities that included Ed Sullivan, Liberace, and Jack Benny – or for those simply grabbing a bite after an evening on the town, Bens was the place to go.

Back in 1908, Lithuanian immigrant Benjamin Kravitz and his wife Fanny established a sweet shop on Montreal's Saint Lawrence Boulevard. Not long afterward, Ben borrowed his mother's recipe and began making smoked meat sandwiches that he sold to neighbourhood workers. Two moves later, the delicatessen opened in 1950 in a new $175,000 building located at the corner of De Maisonneuve and Metcalf Street. From this location a few blocks south of McGill University, Bens continued to serve customers 23 hours a day (one hour needed for cleaning) until it closed in 2006 after its employees – unionized in 1995 – went on strike.

Despite intense efforts from heritage groups to preserve the building intact, or at least have it incorporated into a new structure, the Bens building was demolished in 2008 – and replaced by a high-rise hotel.

Fortunately, not everything from Bens has disappeared; portions of its exterior signage were salvaged and are now on permanent display in a Concordia University stairwell. As well, many artifacts that were saved by Ben's grandson were featured in a 2014 exhibition at the McCord Museum that included a re-creation of the restaurant's photographic 'Wall of Fame.' Naturally, the Museum's café sold smoked-meat sandwiches made from the original recipe.

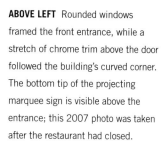

ABOVE LEFT Rounded windows framed the front entrance, while a stretch of chrome trim above the door followed the building's curved corner. The bottom tip of the projecting marquee sign is visible above the entrance; this 2007 photo was taken after the restaurant had closed.

TOP Yellow counters and tabletops, polished chrome stools with incised speed stripes, yellow laminate walls, brushed chrome backsplashes, and a terrazzo floor with yellow and green diamonds all helped create the quintessential diner atmosphere. The all-male waiters wore white shirts with a black bowtie, black trousers and shoes, and a white waist apron. Notice the hooks for diners' jackets beneath the curved counter.

ABOVE RIGHT Although a later example of the Streamlined Moderne style, the three-storey brick building's façade boasted multiple planes, ribbon windows, and a large curved corner. The ground-floor window at the far end of the main façade featured a large curve, echoing the round columns just inside the front entrance. The fascia signage seen here is not the original; a 1965 video shows a series of individual letters that were illuminated from within.

LIFE ON THE
MOVE

This chapter presents buildings and structures associated with travel between the wars. It opens with places where journeys started or finished – bus terminals, railway stations and airports – then moves on to service stations, and bridges, which helped motorists reach their destinations. Finally, the chapter concludes with several hotels, where travellers were greeted with a warm welcome at the end of the day.

Central Station, Toronto, Hamilton & Buffalo Railway Company

36 Hunter Street East, Hamilton, Ontario

Fellheimer & Wagner (New York), 1930–33

Before automobiles became popular and air travel arrived on the scene, people and goods in the newly formed Dominion of Canada were primarily transported by water or by rail.

When it became clear, in the 1870s, that Toronto would become the commercial centre of Ontario, Hamilton decided that attracting industry was the key to its future prosperity. By the mid-1880s, it was already a stop on the Great Western Railway's route connecting Niagara Falls and Windsor. And thanks to its existing port facilities and the arrival of affordable electricity in 1896, Hamilton was soon home to a wide range of manufacturing companies.

The Toronto, Hamilton & Buffalo Railway Company, which commenced operations in 1892, provided these manufacturers with an alternative to the Grand Truck Railway when shipping their products to Canadian customers in Toronto and beyond, and to those in the U.S. TH&B was acquired three years later by the Canadian Pacific Railway and the New York Central Railway.

By 1930, the railway decided it needed a new passenger terminal. Seasoned railroad station designers and architects Fellheimer & Wagner had just completed the magnificent, 17-storey, Zigzag-style Central Terminal in nearby Buffalo. Their initial design for the TH&B station involved a 10-storey, stepped-back tower with flanking wings. However, the arrival of the Depression caused the plans to be scaled back to the sleek, seven-storey structure that exists today.

The station's double-height, curved waiting area included rounded glass corners flanking the front entrance, streamlined wooden benches, and a geometrically patterned terrazzo floor. Polished metal lettering above the northwest entrance presented an abbreviated version of the company's name, set in a sophisticated 1930s typeface.

After TH&B ceased using the station in 1981, the building lay empty – although its historical value was recognized in 1994 with a designation under the Ontario Heritage Act. Following extensive renovations, the Streamlined Moderne building reopened in 1996 as the city's GO Transit bus and train station.

ABOVE Clad in smooth panels of Queenston limestone, the steel-frame, seven-storey structure was essentially free of decoration. The building's design combined Zigzag and Streamlined Moderne elements: its step-back massing and central band of vertical windows complemented the horizontally proportioned wraparound windows and the rounded corners on the flanking two-storey wings. Notice the semicircular canopy over the front entrance, and the wing-like detailing beneath the flagpole brackets.

Toronto Coach Terminal

610 Bay Street, Toronto, Ontario
Charles Brammall Dolphin, 1931

The rapid growth in bus travel in the late 1920s prompted the Toronto Transportation Commission – the predecessor to today's Toronto Transit Commission – to replace its open-air terminal at the corner of Bay and Edward Streets with a new, enclosed motor coach terminal in the same location.

The new block-long facility was carefully planned to avoid congestion, with coaches entering from Elizabeth Street and loading at a series of covered platforms that exited onto Edward Street. Walking into the new terminal building from Bay Street, passengers first purchased their tickets at the main floor ticket counter, then sat on padded wooden benches in the two-storey waiting room. If they chose, they could patronize the newsstand, cigar store, or drug store, or climb the marble staircase to a lounge area on the open mezzanine level. The remaining space on the second floor housed rental offices. The ladies' washroom was on the main level; the basement level housed the mens' washroom, a shoeshine stand, and storage space. The southern wall of the waiting area featured two maps: one of the city; the other of southern Ontario, displaying the routes served by the five separate bus lines using the terminal.

The facility was officially opened on December 19, 1931, by the province's acting premier. Toronto Mayor William James Stewart then purchased, but did not use, the terminal's first ticket for a return trip to Hamilton. Before the coach's departure, he climbed aboard and wished everyone a Merry Christmas.

A 1990 renovation retained most of the building's features; at present, the terminal's seven platforms – and those in an adjacent structure – serve over one million passengers annually travelling to cities throughout Ontario and the northeastern U.S.

RIGHT The double-height, arched entrance portal facing Bay Street contributed to the two-storey, limestone-clad building's Stripped Classical styling, although the step-back detailing atop its pilasters lent a Zigzag touch. The original doors and window frames were aluminum with a satin finish.

ABOVE LEFT Continuous recesses in the multiple-plane pilasters enhanced the main façade's sense of verticality, as did the vertical stripes in the cast-aluminum spandrel panels that originally had a brush finish with polished highlights. Notice the smooth traditional dentils that adorned the roofline.

TOP This view of the elegant interior shows the lounge area on the north side of the mezzanine, accessed by the grand T-shaped staircase. The Stripped Classical squared and fluted columns that supported the ceiling beams were clad in travertine. On the main level, separate doors served arriving and departing passengers. In addition to a central frosted-glass skylight, the interior was illuminated by five Zigzag-style chandeliers that were described in a period journal as being of "agreeable modern design in ivory glass and aluminum." The stained-glass window at the stair landing, containing the Gray Coach Lines logo, is still present today.

City of Toronto Archives, Fonds 16, Series 71, Item 9035.

Provincial Transport Company Bus Terminal

1188 Dorchester Street West (now René-Lévesque Boulevard), Montreal, Quebec

Shorey & Ritchie, 1938 (demolished)

Incorporated in November 1928, the Provincial Transport Company soon purchased and consolidated 31 mostly owner-operated bus lines based in outlying communities that each brought passengers into Montreal. An early advertisement for the company noted that "our luxurious coaches – cool and breezy in summer, comfortably heated in winter – operate to most of the important points in the Province of Quebec and make connections for major cities in the United States and Canada."

A new terminal became necessary as passenger traffic grew; in October 1937, a rendering of the facility was published in the *Montreal Gazette*. The building was situated where the American Presbyterian Church once stood – close to the city's hotels, commercial district, and main railway stations. Although not completely finished, the company began using the terminal on May 2, 1938.

The new terminal building provided all the amenities needed by the travelling public. In addition to the usual waiting room, ticket counter, and baggage area, the main floor contained a travel bureau and a circular information desk – as well as a U-shaped lunch counter that dispensed sodas and sundaes on one side while selling cigars and other merchandise on the other. Washrooms, a shoeshine parlour, drivers' room, and extra baggage storage were located in the basement; the upper two floors housed company offices. The covered platform extending out from the rear led to the 20 coach bays. The terminal building was set well back from Dorchester Street to allow cars and taxis to easily drop-off and pick-up passengers.

Regrettably, the inevitable march of time led to the demolition of this attractive and functional structure.

RIGHT Above the glass-block walls enclosing the ticket counter was a bas-relief mural that a period journal described as "depicting speed, safety, power and luxury co-ordinated."

TOP The three-storey Streamlined Moderne building, clad in buff-coloured brick, was dominated by two design elements. The first was the curved extension to the parapet at the building's northwest corner that helped support the large bilingual sign. The second was the pair of ribbon windows that stretched across the upper floors; these were subdivided by four narrow strips of dark-coloured tile that marked the location of the columns within. The building was well identified with signage: the company initials were displayed at the base of the rooftop flagpole; freestanding letters spelled out the company name atop the rounded-corner canopy; and the Greyhound Lines logo and sprinting dog symbol were centred on the north façade.

ABOVE This view of the waiting room reveals the spaciousness of the main floor. The walls were painted a greenish-yellow colour; the pattern of concentric squares in the floor was aligned with the tall, smoothly finished concrete columns. In addition to windows on two sides, the waiting room was lit by cove lighting in the ceiling plus lamps atop the information desk's central column. Two circular glass-block windows on the main façade enhanced the interior's Streamlined character.

Greyhound Bus Station

40 London Avenue East (now University Avenue), Windsor, Ontario

Sheppard & Masson; Bonfield & Cumming (Cleveland, associates), 1940

Back in 1850, public transit in the Windsor area consisted of horse-drawn stagecoaches that transported people to the popular sulphur hot springs in the small town of Sandwich, some five kilometres away. This evolved, in 1872, into a horse-drawn streetcar system, operated by the Sandwich, Windsor & Amherstburg (SW&A) Railway Company. With assistance in the 1920s from the Hydro-Electric Power Commission of Ontario, some rail routes were converted to electrically powered, trackless trolley cars that carried 29 passengers. But when this service quickly proved to be insufficient, the system was converted to electric-powered streetcars running on tracks.

In the late 1930s, Windsor made a rapid transition from streetcars to motor coaches, completing the process in just 14 months; some of the then-unused streetcars were shipped to South America. The conversion to buses meant that a new station was needed to serve both local bus routes as well as inter-city coaches.

Built across the street from the red-brick Armouries of 1900, the Greyhound station was two storeys tall at the front, with a one-storey canopy extending out from the rear to shelter the bus bays. SW&A – reorganized as Windsor Transit in 1977 – operated out of the building until 2007, when it moved to a newly built facility a few blocks west.

In the late 1970s, the lower portion of the exterior was unfortunately concealed behind gravel-textured panels, while the upper level was covered in ungainly vertical metal siding.

At present, the vacant building is owned by the University of Windsor; plans have been announced that would retain and restore the front curved portion of the façade and construct new academic facilities behind.

ABOVE The front façade of the two-storey Streamlined Moderne station was faced with limestone above a black granite base. Like other Greyhound stations being built in the U.S., this building featured smoothly rounded corners and a vertical neon sign emblazoned with the company name and topped by a cutout version of the racing greyhound. Beneath the sign was a generous canopy – also with rounded corners – whose chrome fascia bore neon-lit speed stripes. Rounded-corner walls and shop windows flanked the front entrance. The offices on the second floor looked out onto the street through metal sash windows with semicircular outer ends; delicate streamlined banding accented the roofline. The sides and rear of the building were sheathed in yellow brick.

Canadian National Railways Central Station

1188 Dorchester Street West (now René-Lévesque Boulevard), Montreal, Quebec

John Schofield; concourse level by John Campbell Merrett, 1942–43

After having been established through the 1919 amalgamation of the Grand Trunk Railway and several other railways, the new, government-owned Canadian National Railways (CNR) had to contend with a series of unconnected tracks and terminals within the City of Montreal. For example, passengers coming from north of the city and wishing to continue in a southwesterly direction to Toronto would need to make a 100-kilometre detour – northwest to Hawkesbury, Ontario – in order to make the connection. CNR eventually resolved the situation by taking advantage of an existing tunnel and building an elevated viaduct, with all tracks terminating at a single new downtown station.

Construction of the new facility first began in 1926, but was put on hold four years later due to the Depression. Work resumed in 1939 on a scaled-back plan, with the new CNR Central Station finally opening on July 14, 1943.

Considered a combination of the Streamlined Moderne style and the new, unadorned International Style, the new station was initially surrounded by open space that was used for taxi drop-offs and parking. But due to the intensification of the area and the construction of surrounding buildings over the intervening decades, the station is now hemmed-in on all sides.

At the heart of Central Station was the concourse – the primary space used by the CNR's passengers. More than 100 metres in length by 30 metres in width, this giant room was illuminated by long stretches of bronze-framed, frosted-glass windows on either side, plus taller end windows whose gently sloped tops matched the symmetrical slopes of the ceiling. Giant ceiling trusses enabled the concourse to be free of columns, with their only structural expression being angled fins along the outer walls – clad in soft blue terrazzo – that subdivided the side windows. Occupying the centre of the concourse – surfaced in red terrazzo – were seven sets of stairs leading down to the rail platforms.

A period journal noted that the station contained "all the facilities to speed passengers on their journeys and many 'extras' that are surely an innovation in railway station design." Beyond the expected amenities of a ticket counter and telegraph office, waiting room, restaurant, soda bar, baggage services, and immigration, the station's 'extras' included bath facilities in the women's washroom – clad in 'shell-pink' and black vitrolite – along with access to a quiet room and attached nursery, and an

ABOVE This 2015 view of the southeast corner of the station reveals the bands of bas-reliefs that stretch across three façades of the station. The area surrounding this side of the building was once level with the concourse; subsequent filling-in means that the base of the concourse windows are now at street level.

ABOVE Rising five stories above the parking level on its main (north) side, the flat-roofed, steel-frame building was clad in grey-brown brick, with gray limestone used for window and door trim, as well as the coping. The Streamlined Moderne elements on this main façade included the upper floors' horizontally proportioned windows that were treated as continuous bands, and the uninterrupted stone trim that framed the large windows above the broad canopy. The three, heroically themed bas-reliefs on the front façade depicted (from left) Mercury, Prometheus and Neptune. This front façade is now almost completely obscured by the 1967 Place Bonaventure mixed-use complex.

Canadian National Railways Central Station

infirmary. The men's washroom provided direct access to a barbershop; away from the concourse was a special area for men in uniform that was operated by the Canadian Legion and contained a lounge, reading and writing room, and a kitchen.

The most spectacular part of the building for Art Deco lovers is the extensive collection of bas-reliefs that adorn both the exterior and interior walls of the building. The 20 external carvings on the east, south, and west walls were designed by Charles Comfort and executed by sculptor Fritz Brandtner; the murals encircling the concourse were also designed by Comfort but executed by sculptor Sebastiano Aiello.

The same period journal recites Comfort's intention for the interior murals: "The work is an effort to formalize the contemporary life of Canadians, their industry, their recreation, their culture, their hopes and aspirations, and to some extent their environment." The bas-reliefs are located in the four corners of the concourse, with each one wrapping around the corner. Beneath the murals are the French and English lyrics of 'O Canada,' which had become the country's de facto national anthem in the latter part of the 1930s.

Central Station was recognized under the federal government's Heritage Railway Station's Protection Act in 1995.

Today, the station is connected to Montreal's Metro system, and is a key stop on the country's most-travelled rail corridor between Windsor and Quebec City. It is also a major hub for commuters living outside the downtown core; current figures estimate that some 11 million people pass through the station each year.

RIGHT This tower at the building's northeast end, and its twin at the opposite end, contained staircases and elevators to reach the upper floors. The recessed brick speed stripes and wraparound windows on the lower block contrast with the vertical band of windows in the taller block. Visible to the right is the bas-relief depicting the god Mercury, seen against a backdrop of commercial activity.

ABOVE The three carved panels above – part of a series of 20 bas-reliefs stretching across the east, south, and west sides of the building – were designed by Charles Comfort and carved by Fritz Brandtner. The seven panels on the building's east façade depicted advancements in transportation by sea; the three panels shown above and a second set of three on the south façade portrayed the evolution of flight; and the seven on the west façade (some now obscured) showcased the history of land transportation. The left-most panel above depicted Wilbur Wright's 1903 flight at Kitty Hawk, North Carolina; the middle panel portrayed the first transatlantic flight in 1919, and the final panel illustrated a Trans-Canada Airlines plane.

RIGHT This contemporary view looking west down the station's concourse shows the large fins that supported the sloping roof. The right-hand section of the giant window at the end of the concourse is now artificially lit, since this portion of the building has been enclosed by new construction. The central sets of stairs and escalators down to the platform level are now largely obscured by seating and signage; the former restaurant space at the western end has been converted to retail space.

TOP LEFT This bas-relief faces east, and presents interlocking images from life in the 'South' of Canada. Among these scenes are a farmer harvesting crops, a man golfing, a woman teaching a young child, a vineyard and apple tree, a locomotive, and men working on the railroad.

ABOVE The figures in this 'West' bas-relief include a cowboy on a bucking bronco, a trio of a fisherman, farmer, and lumberjack, a prospector panning for gold, a woman picking apples, and a West Coast First Nations man in ceremonial dress, standing in front of a totem pole.

Introduction to Airport Buildings

Renowned Scottish-born inventor Alexander Graham Bell and four others were responsible for the first successful flight in Canada, which took place in Nova Scotia on February 23, 1909. Flying at an altitude of between three and nine metres, the Silver Dart 'heavier-than-air machine' travelled nearly one kilometre over frozen Baddeck Bay on Cape Breton Island.

Four years later, bundles of newspapers were transported by air from Montreal to Ottawa, marking the first commercial cargo flight; the first airmail delivery took place in 1919, when a Boeing-made aircraft carried 60 letters from Vancouver's Coal Harbour to Seattle. Regularly scheduled passenger service began in 1920, when Imperial Oil shuttled men and supplies from Edmonton to the remote oil fields in Fort Norman (now Tulita) in the Northwest Territories.

Over 23,000 Canadian airmen, including ace Billy Bishop, flew with British air forces during World War I; after the war, many helped set up recreational flying clubs and associations in towns across the country. At these early airports (also known as aerodromes or air harbours), the airstrips were rarely paved or equipped with lighting. In 1928, the federal government began providing financial assistance to local flying clubs to upgrade their facilities, ushering in a network known as the Trans-Canada Airway. As a Depression relief project, Prime Minister R.B. Bennett initiated the construction of new airfields located 80 kilometres apart between Lethbridge, Lethbridge and Vancouver, which proved beneficial during World War II.

In 1926, grain merchant James A. Richardson formed Winnipeg-based Western Canadian Airways (later renamed Canadian Airways Limited); its northern flights – known as 'bush flying' – helped expand the country's mining industry. Concerned about the encroachment of American airline interests, federal cabinet minister C.D. Howe helped engineer the formation of the country's first national airline – Trans-Canada Air Lines Limited – in 1937 as a subsidiary of the government-owned Canadian National Railways. TCA commenced transcontinental passenger and scheduled mail services on April 1, 1939. Three years later, CNR's competitor, Canadian Pacific Railways, entered the airline business as Canadian Pacific Air Lines.

Airport facilities were required to serve the increase in passenger and freight traffic; this resulted in the improvement of runway facilities and the construction of airport terminals across Canada in the late 1930s and 1940s. Three of these buildings are profiled in the following pages.

Causeway Tower & Garage

812 Wharf Street, Victoria, British Columbia
Townley & Matheson, 1930–31

Situated right on the shore of the Inner Harbour in downtown Victoria – a short walk from the B.C. Legislature and the legendary Empress Hotel – the Causeway Tower & Garage was the flagship downtown service station for Imperial Oil. The lower two floors of the three-storey structure housed the station's service bays, with room for 120 automobiles; facilities were also provided for mooring watercraft. The building opened for business on June 19, 1931.

The building served a second purpose: as an aircraft signalling tower. During the Depression, Canada's West Coast experienced relative prosperity compared to the Prairies, where financially strapped families stopped driving their cars altogether, or converted them to 'Bennett buggies' – vehicles without engines that were pulled by horses. Victoria's leaders – inspired by Charles Lindbergh's 1927 New York-to-Paris flight – sought to transform the Inner Harbour into a landing area for seaplanes; some even believed that air travel would overtake travel on land! Against this optimistic backdrop, it is little wonder that the 25-metre, Zigzag-style signalling tower was constructed atop the service station. Crowning the tower was a rotating Sperry beacon; visible almost 100 kilometres away, the beacon went dark at the start of World War II.

The service station was closed in 1975; the building now houses a Visitor's Information Centre. It was granted a Municipal Heritage Designation in 1986.

ABOVE LEFT This period photo shows the early days of the building when it was a service station. The red-tile roofs sheltered the sheltered the street-level gas pump island as well as the main gas station structure; this Spanish Colonial Revival treatment aimed to evoke the era's glamorous lifestyle seen in Hollywood movies.

ABOVE RIGHT The striking, reinforced concrete tower displays the essential characters of the Zigzag style: symmetrical step-back massing, multiple planes, and geometric detailing. The protruding ribbed panels on its four corners enhance the sense of verticality; the top of the tower features a narrow band of recessed fluting. The clock faces and banner supports on its four faces were added within the past quarter-century.

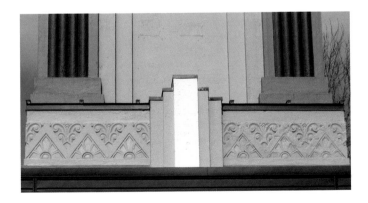

ABOVE The base of the tower is adorned with typical Zigzag sunbursts and floral motifs. The tower's colours have changed over the years as it has been repainted.

United Services Corporation Garage

5600 Sackville Street, Halifax, Nova Scotia
Sydney Perry Dumaresq, 1937 (demolished 2016)

Through his parent company United Services Corporation, Halifax-based businessman Fred C. Manning owned a vast array of enterprises rivalling those of legendary New Brunswick entrepreneur K.C. Irving. Manning's empire – which prospered in spite of the Depression – consisted of bus lines, trucking companies, wholesale automotive supplies, car dealerships, and a network of service stations throughout Nova Scotia and New Brunswick.

Erected at the southeast corner of an important downtown intersection facing the historic Halifax Citadel, this $150,000 multi-purpose building was the centre of Manning's empire. The ground floor housed a General Motors showroom featuring the latest Oldsmobiles and Chevrolets; the upper two floors contained the company's offices. Manning's rounded-corner office – and that of his private secretary – was panelled with inlaid mahogany specially imported from Venezuela; it included a private bathroom and shower, as well as a concealed liquor cabinet.

In addition to gas pumps, the lower level of the building contained facilities for maintaining and repairing cars. Since space on the corner lot was at a premium, parking – with room for 40 cars – was located on the reinforced-concrete structure's roof, which was accessed via a custom-built 'auto elevator.'

In 1942, a few years after Manning sold his business, the Canadian Broadcasting Corporation (CBC) leased the building to serve as the headquarters of its Halifax operations. Transmission towers were soon installed on its roof. It was in these studios that Canadian broadcasting legend Max Ferguson, who had joined the local radio station as a staff announcer at station CBH in 1946, created his much-loved on-air character 'Old Rawhide.' Various local cultural groups were also given free office space in the building.

CBC finally purchased the building in the early 1980s, but was forced to sell it in 2014 as a result of budgetary challenges and facility consolidation.

After it was acquired by a local development company, the building began to be demolished in March 2016. The site will soon house a multi-storey condominium complex, with the new structure's lower floors housing an expanded YMCA.

ABOVE The building is seen here in 2012, prior to CBC's departure and its 2016 demolition.

TOP Seen here in a trade advertisement shortly after it opened, the reinforced concrete building was finished with white cement – specially imported from England – to help the imposing structure appear less massive. Its bold rounded corner with horizontally proportioned windows contributes to its Streamlined Moderne character. The ground floor 'drive-through' enabled automobiles to access the service bays, as well as the rooftop parking area.

York Hotel

636 Centre Street Southeast, Calgary, Alberta
Jacob Knoepfli (designer), 1929–30 (disassembled 2007)

The corner of Seventh Avenue and Centre Street in downtown Calgary once housed Knox Presbyterian Church, and later, the city's first oil exchange building. But in the late 1920s, Builders and Investors Limited – led by president Jacob Knoepfli – purchased the property and spent some $650,000 to erect the York Hotel. Formerly a carpenter from Ontario who moved to Calgary in 1905, Knoepfli designed the building himself, and reportedly hired a Hollywood studio artist named E. Merrill Owens to craft the remarkable Zigzag-style panels located above the first floor and at the roofline of the southern and western façades.

At the time that Mayor Andrew Davison opened the 187-room hotel on April 2, 1930, it contained a boardroom for business meetings, bowling lanes, billiards tables, a beer parlour – as well as a ladies lounge and hair salon. With its blazing neon sign, the York was described as the 'modern hotel,' in contrast to Knoepfli's 'family hotel,' later known as the St. Regis, located two doors to the east. The hotel's second floor housed CFCN Radio – the 'Voice of the Prairies' – from which 'Bible Bill' Aberhart delivered his weekly broadcasts.

The hotel's story has been full of twists and turns since its early days. A 1968 full-page newspaper ad proclaimed its reopening after a complete refurbishment, yet a fire only two years later required a $1-million renovation. In 1984, a *Calgary Herald* story reported that 35 employees would be out of work after the building's two strip bars were unexpectedly closed. Three years later, almost 80 long-term residents of the hotel nearly faced eviction to make room for officials from the 1988 Olympics. In 1993, the structure's future seemed secure when it was purchased by the city and converted to affordable housing.

In the mid-2000s, the York Hotel property was acquired as part of the development of The Bow, Calgary's landmark skyscraper. Disassembly of the Category C designated building commenced in the summer of 2007, with its bricks being salvaged while cranes carefully lifted sawn sections of the Art Deco frieze. The project's plans called for the building's southern and western façades – complete with the dazzling friezes – to be rebuilt as part of the second phase of The Bow project, but Calgary's economic downturn has left the project currently unfinished.

ABOVE The prominent southern and western façades of the eight-storey hotel building were clad in brown brick from the Clayburn Brick Company east of Vancouver; the other two façades employed less expensive brick. While easily mistaken for terracotta, the building's decorative friezes above the first and eighth floors were actually made of solid concrete that was cast in molds at the same time as the building's reinforced concrete structure, then painted in earth tones to complement the brick.

ABOVE The motifs in the building's decorative friezes are quintessential Deco – fiddlehead scrolls, plant fronds, chevrons, and segments of circles. The vertical groove in the middle of the decorative slab was actually a saw-cut in the solid concrete to make the panel appear more like terracotta.

Hotels

Sussex Hotel

1001 Douglas Street, Victoria, British Columbia
Studley Patrick Birley, 1938 (façade retained 1997)

After Vancouver was selected as the western terminus of the Canadian Pacific Railway in 1886, the City of Victoria decided to trade upon its natural beauty and mild climate in establishing a civic image of refinement and tradition. Its coastal location helped make the city an appealing destination for tourists travelling by automobile or arriving by ferry.

Erected only a few blocks from the harbour, the sophisticated Sussex Hotel set out to attract these motoring travellers; its initial plans even called for a drive-through in its southern façade to access a parking lot behind. Entering its chamfered corner entrance, guests passed through a rectangular vestibule to the octagonal elevator lobby. Into the mid-1980s, the hotel's interior was mostly intact; in 1995, the building was added to the city's Community Heritage Register.

The structure's inner sections were demolished in 1997, with the two principal façades being retained as part of an adjacent 11-storey building project. The windows and spandrels near the entrance were removed and replaced by open, geometric grilles to create a skylit, two-storey entrance court.

TOP A series of two-tone, frozen-fountain glazed panels formed the base of each brick pier. Notice the horizontally ridged, tan-coloured tiles that stretched across the two principal façades.

BOTTOM The brick piers defining the chamfered corner entrance – as well as the horizontal and vertical neon signs – feature multiple-plane, step-back detailing.

MIDDLE Seen here in 1992, after the hotel had closed but prior to its partial demolition, the three-storey building displayed many aspects of the Zigzag style. The windows on the upper two floors of the red-brick façades were treated as vertical strips, with herringbone-patterned brickwork forming the spandrels. Between each window, the parapet was adorned with multiple-plane, vertical bands of brick that terminated in a small step-back element. Dividing each grouping of three windows were more pronounced, protruding-brick piers that were crowned with large step-backs.

LIFE OF
LEISURE

This final chapter showcases the movie theatres in which Canadians escaped their everyday lives and entered the glamorous world of their favourite Hollywood stars. It also features several arenas where people cheered on their sports heroes, and auditoriums where the period's leading performers practised their craft.

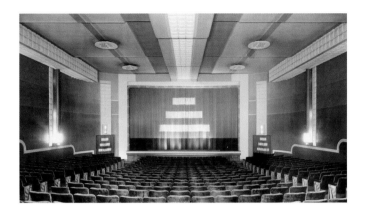

Introduction to Movie Theatres

In the days before TV and the internet, Canadians seeking entertainment outside the home could either visit majestic theatres to enjoy 'serious' fare such as dramas, operas, and ballet performances, or take in lower-priced vaudeville shows in less formal surroundings.

Although moving pictures first appeared within a diverse vaudeville lineup, they came into their own during the first two decades of the twentieth century. The earliest moving-picture theatres in Canada were small and inexpensively built structures. Next came larger 'deluxe' movie houses, as well as the more lavish movie palaces that arrived in the first half of the 1920s. Often featuring classical décor, these theatres contained impressive organs, orchestra pits for the musicians who accompanied the silent films, as well as comfortable and elegantly appointed lounges.

The latter half of the 1920s saw the introduction of 'atmospheric' theatres, in which the configuration and decoration of the auditorium and foyer sought to magically transport audiences to exotic destinations. Cove-lit ceilings were painted blue to resemble the sky, sometimes including twinkling lights; auditorium walls were usually decorated to look like castles, courtyards, or gardens.

The introduction of sound to moving pictures in the late 1920s – the 'talkies' – meant that the elaborate décor of the atmospherics gave way to simpler cinema interiors, as moviegoers focused more on the screen and less on the visual impression of the theatre itself.

The onset of the Depression meant that while the larger downtown cinemas still attracted audiences, neighbourhood cinemas – the 'nabes' – grew in popularity. People could walk a few blocks from their home and take a seat in a comfortable – and often air-conditioned – auditorium, enjoying an affordable escape from the burdens of everyday life. The cost of going to the movies dropped dramatically at this time, with kids shelling out only a dime on a Saturday afternoon to watch two features that were interspersed with trailers, newsreels, cartoons, and serials.

The design of movie theatres evolved as they began to incorporate – inside and out – the sleek surfaces and bold shapes appearing in the lavish film sets on the screen. The era of the Art Deco movie theatre had arrived. The country's leading cinema designers in the 1930s and 1940s were architects Harold Kaplan and Abraham Sprachman, who reportedly designed 80 percent of the country's movie theatres.

In a 1938 period journal article, Samuel 'Roxy' Rothafel – the American theatre impresario best known for opening Radio City Music Hall in New York City – was quoted as saying: "Theatre entertainment, by my definition, takes place, not only on the stage, but at the box office, in the lobby, the foyer, the rest rooms, and the auditorium itself. Once within the doors of the theatre, the purchaser of a ticket becomes a guest of the management, and the management's simple duty is to entertain him until he leaves."

But beginning in the 1950s, the entertainment options of Canadians widened. Cinemas faced competition from television sets in living rooms, movie rentals, specialty TV channels, multiplex cinemas – and today, online streaming. As a result, all the movie-theatre buildings in this section have taken on new uses.

Empress Theatre

5560 Sherbrooke Street West, Montreal, Quebec
Joseph-Alcide Chaussé, 1927

Located in the desirable, middle-class Montreal neighbourhood of Notre-Dame-de-Grâce, the Empress Theatre straddled the era of 'atmospheric' theatres and that of more conventional Art Deco movie-houses. However, what set this structure apart was its decoration: it was the country's only cinema adorned – inside and out – with neo-Egyptian styling. In keeping with the adventuresome spirit of the Roaring Twenties, the Empress's design embodied the worldwide interest in the motifs of Ancient Egypt.

Constructed for Confederation Amusements Limited, the 1,550-seat theatre was formally opened in 1928 by Montreal Mayor Camilien Houde. It initially served as a venue for vaudeville and burlesque performances as well as films, but later became a full-time, double-bill cinema after the arrival of 'talkies.' A distinctive feature of the building was its extensive fireproofing, including its ornate asbestos fire curtain.

The mastermind of the Empress's ubiquitous Egyptian interior décor was Malta-born theatre decorator Emmanuel Briffa, who was involved in almost all Montreal theatre projects over three decades. The carvings on the exterior were the handiwork of Montreal sculptor Edward Galea.

Over the next half-century, the Empress's configuration, name, and repertoire evolved to meet changing tastes. In 1962, it became a Vegas-style dinner theatre operating as Royal Follies; three years later, its balcony was turned into a separate auditorium, and it was rechristened the *Cinema V-Salle Hermes.* During the subsequent two decades, it went from screening adult fare to art-house films before finally becoming a thriving repertory theatre. Famous Players purchased the building in 1988 and filled its screens with first-run films until a 1992 fire damaged the interior, forcing its closure.

Chain-link fencing was erected around the building to protect it from vandals; the City of Montreal took ownership of the structure in 1999. A coalition of arts groups put forward a plan in 2009 to revive the building, but the provincial government withdrew its offer to fund half the project, and the theatre's ownership reverted to the city. A local group established to restore the deteriorating structure and transform it into a cultural and community centre was unable to raise sufficient funds to meet the city's deadline, leaving the building's future uncertain.

TOP Made of artificial stone finished to resemble sandstone, the façade of the four-storey, reinforced-concrete theatre was carefully designed and carved to resemble an Ancient Egyptian temple. Flanking the entrance were giant ornate pilasters; tapered columns, bas-reliefs of papyrus fans and giant birds, plus incised hieroglyphs decorated other parts of the façade.

RIGHT Seen here in 2015, the exterior of the vacant building is fundamentally intact, although surrounded by a chain-link fence to help protect it from further damage.

ABOVE RIGHT A period journal noted that the auditorium, painted in shades of red, blue, silver, and gold, "has the effect of a court of an Egyptian palace. On the upper walls there is a series of painted panels of views of the River Nile, framed in pillars as though glimpsed from a building on its banks." The courtyard scene extended far into the distance on the painted fire curtain. Adorned with motifs of lotus leaves, the rectangular enclosures on either side of the proscenium arch concealed the pipes of the house organ. The sky-blue domed ceiling was decorated with pale stars.

ABOVE LEFT This contemporary view of one of the tall pilasters shows an Egyptian male rendered in the distinctive pose: flat torso, with head and feet facing forward. Opposite him is a woman wearing a vulture headdress. Visible above and below them are representations of lotus and palm leaves; crowning the pilaster is a realistic carving of a pharaoh's head topped by the sacred hooded cobra.

Castle Theatre

6956 St. Denis Street, Montreal, Quebec

René Charbonneau, 1931

Known to Montrealers as *Le Chateau*, this 1,300-seat cinema was the last movie-house to be constructed in the city for more than five years, on account of the Depression. Like the 1927 Empress Theatre, this expensive movie-house was built for Confederation Amusements, but designed by a different architect, René Charbonneau.

Opened on Christmas Eve 1931, *Le Chateau* sat across the street from the Rivoli, designed five years earlier in a neoclassical style. Two shops occupied its street-corners; as of 1936, these were Château Sweets and a shoeshine parlour.

The theatre's decoration was very much in the Art Deco realm, but with a generous helping of French sophistication. The front façade's extensive carvings were created by Joseph Guardo, a talented artist who painted and carved both religious and secular works for a range of clients. The extravagant interior was the work of Emmanuel Briffa, in this instance demonstrating his fluency in the lush, floral language of Zigzag styling.

The building originally featured a large projecting sign that was located above a marquee made to resemble a stone castle topped by crenellations. The building is now on its fourth marquee, this one for the building's present occupant, the Metropolitan Christian Centre.

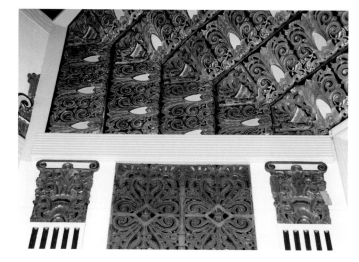

TOP Traversing the entire cast-stone front façade of the building was a crisp, bas-relief wave motif. A series of five slightly bevelled stone piers extended above and below this wave; above, the space between the piers contained carved bas-reliefs of storks and the usual assortment of floral motifs. Below, the piers were adorned with panels of men singing that separated four stained-glass windows with triangular panes. Carvings of allegorical young women flanked the base of the smooth stone arch.

MIDDLE Seen here in 2007, the rectangular proscenium arch consists of five planes of gilded plaster, richly decorated with floral scrolls and lotus leaves.

BOTTOM Combining floral scrolls with subtle chevrons and a sunrise, this silver- and gold-painted plaster detail is located above a main auditorium exit door.

LEFT Located on either side of the front façade were giant stained-glass windows that illuminated the cinema's upper foyer, this one depicting a sunrise. The surrounding carvings, as on other parts of the façade, presented images relating to theatrical entertainment, including the masks of tragedy and comedy, and muses playing musical instruments.

ABOVE This overall view of the three-storey building – seen here in 1989 before its brown-painted façade had been cleaned – reveals its traditional massing; the hangar-like arched section on its north face is echoed in the three segments of the eastern façade that are topped with decorative arches. The base of the building is made of stone, with brown-brick walls above.

Eglinton Theatre

400 Eglinton Avenue West, Toronto, Ontario
Kaplan & Sprachman, 1934

Without doubt, the Eglinton Theatre in Toronto was one of Canada's finest movie-houses. It was developed by an entrepreneurial Sicilian immigrant named Agostino Arrigo, who envisioned a state-of-the-art cinema to serve the residents of the newly incorporated village of Forest Hill.

With financial support from the Famous Players theatre chain, Arrigo retained the services of Kaplan & Sprachman who, at that point, had designed only a handful of cinemas elsewhere in the city but were active in creating apartment buildings and other structures. The plans for the 800-seat Eglinton were drawn up in 1934; three years later, the $200,000 theatre would go on to win a bronze Governor General's medal.

Since the cinema's auditorium ran parallel to the street rather than directly back from the foyer, there was space along the front façade for a series of small shops that would help defray the theatre's operating costs. In 1947, these stores included a barbershop, clothing store, bookstore, and candy shop.

On April 2, 1936 – opening night – hundreds of people from across Toronto lined up at the chrome-and-vitrolite ticket booth. On the bill was *King of Burlesque*, starring Warner Baxter, Alice Faye, and Jack Oakie, which went on to earn an Oscar nomination for best dance direction. Orchestra-level seats on opening night went for 35¢; the best seats on the upper level – where smoking was permitted – cost 10¢ more. The next week, however, orchestra seats dropped to 25¢.

Upon entering the gleaming front doors, moviegoers passed through a mirrored lobby at street level, then descended a few steps into the elegant foyer that featured rounded corners, gleaming metalwork, plush seating, and even a streamlined fireplace. Popcorn in hand, they ascended a flight of steps to the gently raked auditorium, or climbed a few more stairs to the mezzanine's loge seating. Architect Abe Sprachman had attended the 1933–34 Century of Progress exposition in Chicago, which undoubtedly influenced the theatre's leading-edge design.

Over the years, the Eglinton screened some of the century's biggest films, including *The Jolson Story* (1946), *The Sound of Music* (which played for 146 weeks between 1965 and 1967), *Star Wars*, and *Titanic*. For a time, it was considered Famous Players' flagship property.

Unlike most of the larger cinemas of its era, the theatre continued to operate profitably as a single-screen movie-house until 2002, when Famous Players closed its doors. Some say the reason for the closure was the company's unwillingness to modify the theatre to make it fully accessible, while others say the movie chain was consolidating its business at two multi-screen cinemas near Yonge and Eglinton.

Following a spirited but unsuccessful community campaign called 'Save the Eglinton Theatre,' the building was acquired by a hospitality and entertainment enterprise that partially restored and remodelled the space as an event venue, reopening it as The Eglinton Grand.

ABOVE LEFT The ticket booth's original detailing is still intact: a red vitrolite base, with streamlined chrome bands framing the semicircular window.

ABOVE RIGHT The cinema's towering pylon, displaying the theatre's name in elegant 1930s lettering outlined in neon, remains intact, as seen in this 2009 photo that was shot after the theatre had been converted to an event space.

OPPOSITE This 1947 view reveals the original Streamlined Moderne styling of the theatre's façade. Contrasting bands of vitrolite created speed-stripes that adorned the edges of the entry block, as well as sections of the wall above the shops. Sadly, this vitrolite was replaced some years ago by nondescript yellow-and-brown glazed tiles. Notice the series of increasingly protruding, ridged cylinders sandwiched between the matching planes of the sign pylon, whose edges were festooned with lightbulbs. Crowning the pylon was a three-part rectangular shaft topped by a flashing ball, all boldly accented with neon.

Eglinton Theatre

ABOVE LEFT The main lobby, a few steps down from street level, continued the streamlined treatment of the exterior. Horizontal speed-stripes adorned the walls and the ever-present ashtrays; vertical stripes subtly accented the walls and the giant easel announcing the coming attraction. To the left of the mirrored wall niche with a vase of flowers is a 'Wall of Honour' commemorative poster.

ABOVE RIGHT The stepped ceiling planes, together with the horizontal decoration at the base and top of the walls, echoed the slope of the auditorium floor. The bold lines in the ceiling, including the stripes on the air-vent diffusers, directed the moviegoer's eyes to the screen, which was concealed by the decorative curtain within a stepped frame. Large chandeliers, coved ceiling lighting, and stacked bands of frosted glass at either side of the main landing provided the illumination. Notice the naked female figures perched atop the emergency exits flanking the screen.

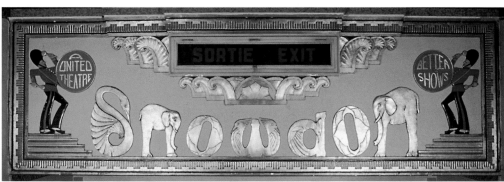

TOP LEFT To help absorb sound, the auditorium's pale blue ceiling featured newly patented 'Heerwagen' acoustic tiles that were arranged in a step-back pattern; at the centre was a long, prism-like light fixture made of steel and glass. Framing the elegantly painted fire curtain were gilded pilasters with clocks, each flanked by air vents in the shape of spider webs. The walls were once painted to resemble bunched drapes – a Briffa favourite.

BOTTOM LEFT This unique sign marked the exit from the auditorium to the foyer. The figures of different animals formed the letters, while the twin marching drums bore the words 'A United Theatre' and 'Better Shows.' A similar marching drummer once appeared in a multicoloured glass panel on the front façade.

TOP RIGHT The plaster molding that surrounded the auditorium was painted silver and gold, and contained the usual array of Zigzag-era sun-rays and floral motifs.

BOTTOM RIGHT This is one of four exotic, bas-relief figures that adorned the auditorium's emergency exits.

Garneau Theatre

8708–8728 109th Street Northwest, Edmonton, Alberta
William George Blakey, 1940

Bill Wilson, the son of a Famous Players theatre manager, assured his wife he'd never take up his father's profession, but after losing his job in 1938, he started raising money for a new chain of theatres. Located southwest of downtown Edmonton, the 780-seat Garneau Theatre was the second cinema opened by his company, Suburban Theatres.

The film on opening night, October 24, 1940, was *The Great Waltz*, the 1938 'biopic' about Viennese composer Johann Strauss II; admission was just 5¢. An article in the *Edmonton Bulletin* explained that "after hanging your coat in the complimentary coat check, a young usher or usherette dressed in a scarlet Eton jacket, blue trousers and black pill box hat will escort you to your seat." The auditorium – which boasted ultramarine walls, blue seats, recessed neon lighting, and a gold-highlighted proscenium arch – also featured a large stage and dressing rooms to accommodate live theatrical performances.

A series of small, street-level stores were incorporated in the building's one-storey front façade; at the rear, rising almost 10 metres, was the two-tone brick block enclosing the auditorium.

In 1941, the theatre was leased to Famous Players, which continued to operate it until the late 1980s. The building was then taken over by Magic Lantern Theatres, which ran it as a discount venue catering to university students. Protests from the community prevented a 1992 redevelopment scheme, and successfully fought off a threatened expropriation by University of Alberta. In 2009, in return for $547,000 in funding from the city, the building's owners agreed to restore the building to its original appearance; it was granted a Municipal Heritage Resource designation that same year.

TOP The theatre's façade is dominated by a symmetrical, stucco-clad, step-back pylon whose bevelled front edge contains the neon-accented cinema name. This verticality is counterbalanced by blue projecting speed-stripes atop the pylon; its wavy front edge boasts a band of lightbulbs that continues down the centre of the bevelled marquee. Notice the built-in ladder rungs flanking the projecting sign.

BOTTOM RIGHT The theatre's name is spelled out in two-tone brickwork on the north and south sides of the auditorium enclosure. Notice the wide bands of darker brick that span the façade, the horizontally proportioned window panes, and the use of glass block.

BOTTOM LEFT Standing behind the one-storey block that housed a series of shops and the cinema entrance was the tall, two-tone brick auditorium enclosure. The façade at street level was faced with Carrara glass and glass block, and boasted stainless-steel-framed doors and windows. The billboards that detract from the majestic marquee were installed in the 1950s.

Broadway Theatre

715 Broadway Avenue, Saskatoon, Saskatchewan
Webster & Gilbert, 1946

Opening on December 5, 1946, the Broadway Theatre was first affiliated with the Odeon movie-theatre chain. But after Famous Players ceased operating the theatre in 1975, it went dark for a couple of years before reopening for a half-decade as an adult film venue. It then switched to screening art-house films and hosting live performances.

Following its sudden closure in August 1993, a public fundraising campaign raised enough money to enable a community non-profit group to purchase and restore the theatre. The Broadway now hosts films, concerts, theatre and dance performances, plus serves as a rental venue. It was recognized as a Municipal Heritage Property in April 1997.

ABOVE This photo shows a standing-room-only cooking school set up on the theatre's stage. Notice how the walls of the auditorium, clad in acoustic tile, stepped back toward the screen, as do the multiple planes directly framing the screen. The streamlined effect is enhanced by the subtle stripes on the front face of the stage, and on the ceiling.

ABOVE LEFT Seen here in 1949, the asymmetrical façade of the two-storey, stucco-clad cinema featured various Streamlined Moderne details. These included the recessed speed-stripes that framed the horizontally proportioned windows on the second floor, the rounded corners flanking the entrance doors, and the glass blocks around the furthest window containing movie posters. Its streamlined pylon sign was topped with curved, neon-lit speed-stripes, while a series of shallow, rounded-top planes adorned its front. The marquee was decorated with a trio of horizontal neon bands, and the usual field of lightbulbs beneath.

Cornwall Theatre

264 LeMarchant Road, St. John's, Newfoundland
McCarter & Colbourne, 1947

As was the custom in post – World War II Newfoundland, this building was constructed of poured-in-place concrete. The Cornwall was outfitted with plush seats, an attractive curtain and screen – and indoor plumbing, an amenity not found in all theatres of the day. It operated as a theatre for little more than a decade; since June 1960, it has been occupied by a plumbing supply business. Both the ground-floor ticket booth and third-floor projection room are now offices, while the main auditorium serves as warehouse space.

ABOVE RIGHT The frontispiece of this three-storey structure featured a series of recessed speed-stripes flanking the second-floor windows; above them stretched a wonderful bas-relief band of chevrons that framed the building date. The windows on the side blocks framed vertically ridged spandrels. The bas-relief crests above these windows featured Zigzag-style triangles, yet the incised theatre initials of 'C' and 'T' were set in old-fashioned type.

Arenas and Auditoriums

Eaton Auditorium

7th Floor, Eaton's College Street Store, 444 Yonge Street, Toronto, Ontario
Jacques Carlu, 1929–30; restored 2001–03

The Eaton Auditorium was designed, built, and restored in concert with the development of the Round Room Restaurant, which was described on page 202.

The hall's opening performance on March 26, 1931, was a multinational affair: Australian soprano Florence Austral and flutist John Amadio were accompanied by Canadian composer and conductor Ernest MacMillan, playing the auditorium's 5,804-pipe, Quebec-made Casavant Frères organ.

Some of the many celebrity musicians that have graced the stage over the years include American jazz legends Duke Ellington and Billie Holiday, tenor Mario Lanza, and crooner Frank Sinatra. In 1945, at just 12 years of age, Canadian prodigy Glenn Gould made his solo debut playing the auditorium's organ; he became so fond of the hall's acoustics that he made many of his later recordings there.

Eaton Auditorium also hosted Kiwanis Music Festivals, early performances by the National Ballet of Canada and the Canadian Opera Company, films, as well as lectures – many about interior decoration to help stimulate sales in the store's home furnishings and lighting departments. A respected British music critic declared in the late 1940s that Eaton Auditorium and the concert hall at Winnipeg's Civic Auditorium (see page 268) were the finest concert halls in Canada; others likened Eaton Auditorium to Carnegie Hall in New York City.

Visitors reached the Seventh Floor by elevator, then stepped into the elegant Streamlined Moderne foyer that featured a box office, cloakroom, and washrooms, as well as the entrances to the auditorium and the Round Room. The auditorium's ground floor seated 795 people on black wooden chairs with beige, imitation-leather backs; an additional 480 people sat on fixed seating in the balcony. One observer described the hall's decoration as "silvered shades of beige and grey with black." Sadly, its acoustics were somewhat compromised in the early 1950s with the installation of a raked floor with fixed seating.

In 1983, Eaton Auditorium Round Room, and foyer were declared a National Historic Site.

After the comprehensive refurbishment that returned Eaton Auditorium to its former glory, it reopened in May 2003 as a key element of The Carlu special event space.

ABOVE Seen here after its main floor was converted to fixed seating, the auditorium's styling was clearly Streamlined Moderne. The backlit, frosted-glass piers flanking the stage and continuing along the ceiling were framed by protruding black horizontal fins. Rounded corners graced the walls flanking the hall's doors, as well as the frosted-glass, chrome-trimmed lights above the doors. The original flooring – now restored – consisted of a giant mosaic pattern of brown and gold linoleum; the original curtain was gold-coloured velour with darker speed-stripes. A music-themed bas-relief topped the proscenium arch.

Auditorium – Ont. – Toronto - College St. Auditorium [1930] (Archives of Ontario, F229-308-0-61-2). Used with permission of Sears Canada Inc.

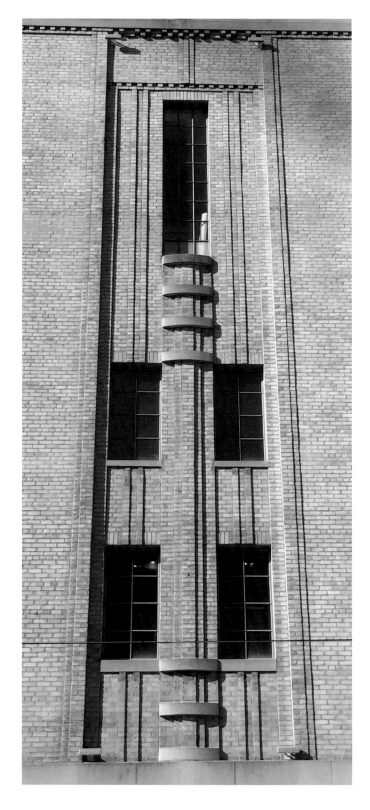

FAR LEFT This taller window is crowned with brick dentils, and features two sets of decorative stone curves that accent the multiple-plane brick pier.

LEFT The stone trim atop this three-storey window resembles a multi-tier ventilation grille, flanked by a pair of M-shaped zigzags.

BOTTOM LEFT This view northward along Church Street reveals the slightly different treatment of the eastern façade. The set of four windows in the corner block illuminated the stairwell.

Civic Auditorium

200 Vaughan Street, Winnipeg, Manitoba
Northwood & Chivers; Pratt & Ross; J. N. Semmens, 1932

This monumental, multi-purpose building – jointly funded by all three levels of government – was developed as a make-work project during the depths of the Depression. Its design work was split between three of the city's leading architectural practices; more interestingly, its construction workers needed to be residents of Winnipeg for at least a year, and either married, or single with dependents. The building materials had to be sourced from greater Winnipeg, or failing that, from elsewhere in Manitoba or at least the British Empire. Prime Minister R.B. Bennett officially opened the building on October 15, 1932.

Operated by a City Committee for nearly four decades – yet earning a profit for only one of those years – the $1-million structure housed five different spaces: an auditorium and concert hall, an art gallery and museum on the second floor, and exhibition galleries flanking the auditorium. Although it seemed like a smart idea to share the stage between the 4,075-seat auditorium and the 800-seat concert hall, it prevented the two spaces from being used simultaneously.

While the auditorium's acoustics were less than perfect, it served as the home of the Winnipeg Symphony Orchestra. Thanks to its flat floor and removable seating, it was an ideal venue for roller-skating, square-dances, wrestling matches, and car shows; Prime Minister John Diefenbaker kicked off his 1958 election campaign there, filling both the auditorium and the concert hall. Later that year, it hosted the first meeting of the Canadian Labour Congress and the Co-operative Commonwealth Federation that led to the formation of the New Democratic Party.

The province acquired the building in 1970; the ensuing renovation removed the auditorium's balconies and installed four floors in the space that, together with the second-floor museum and gallery, now houses the Archives of Manitoba and the Legislative Library. In the latter part of the 1990s, the empty concert hall underwent a similar infill, and now contains the archives of the Hudson's Bay Company.

ABOVE This period view of the main entrance highlights the building's decorative elements. Most prominent were the Zigzag-style capitals that adorned all three faces of the stone piers; immediately above them was a 'dogtooth' decorative band. Flanking the inscribed building name were two octagonal carvings. Notice the decorative pattern in the metal-sash windows, and the octagonal metal light fixtures that dramatically illuminated the façade.

TOP LEFT This heroic-styled carving of a woman cradling a subtly decorated cornucopia clearly reveals the mottled colouration of the building's Tyndall limestone cladding.

LEFT The pre-cast concrete decorative capitals on this side entrance pavilion depicted bundles of corn stalks flanked by scroll motifs. Above were three octagonal carvings: the left one featured a European woman with a cornucopia, the right one portrayed a First Nations hunter, and the central one depicted the provincial crest flanked by doves holding olive branches – perhaps symbolizing the peaceful co-existence of the two peoples. The recessed openings between the piers now contain modern plate-glass windows.

TOP RIGHT The size of this restrained, Zigzag-style building – clad in several varieties of Tyndall limestone – is evident in this period photo. The symmetrical, multiple-plane principal façade is punctuated by five, deeply inset openings that contained doors to the lobby and auditorium foyer, and windows above that brought natural light into the mezzanine's committee rooms and the second floor's assembly hall. On the sides, the arched windows between the two protruding entrance pavilions illuminated the exhibition galleries. Not visible at the rear is the concert hall; behind the gently sloping pediment lay a flat roof.

ABOVE A period journal noted that the auditorium with its cantilevered seating "is characterized by modernity and simplicity." The flooring of the stage and auditorium hall was hardwood, while the walls and ceiling were finished with acoustical plaster. Geometrically patterned grilles surrounded the multiple-plane proscenium arch; the flanking vents resembled corn stalks.

Trois-Rivières Coliseum

1740 Gilles Villeneuve Avenue, Trois-Rivières, Quebec
Jules Caron, 1938

Although first observed by Jacques Cartier on his voyage up the St. Lawrence River in 1535, the area now known as Trois-Rivières gained its first permanent settlement in 1634, at the recommendation of Samuel de Champlain. Its name derives from the fact that the mouth of the south-flowing St. Maurice River contains two islands, creating the impression of three separate rivers. The territory remained under French rule until captured by the British in 1760, as part of the Seven Years' War.

The establishment of an iron foundry back in 1738 was the basis for the community's claim to being the oldest industrial city in Canada. Its port facilities and the 1879 arrival of the railway supported the growth of the lumber industry. A fire in 1908 destroyed much of the city, but the subsequent reconstruction brought new industries and residents to the region, with the population nearly doubling between 1921 and 1941. For three decades near the middle of the century, Trois-Rivières was considered the world capital for pulp-and-paper manufacturing.

The onset of the Depression prompted the local government, in 1931, to launch plans to refurbish the city's exhibition grounds as a make-work program. One element of the project – not actually constructed until 1938 – was a coliseum structure to house public gatherings. Enclosed passageways connected the Coliseum to a pair of flanking exhibition venues, each of which terminated in a three-storey, silo-shaped structure whose interior was illuminated by a ring of clerestory windows. Other components of the exhibition ground's redevelopment program included an outdoor baseball stadium, a sizeable outdoor swimming pool, and the Porte Pacifique-Duplessis entrance gate.

The year after the Coliseum's completion, the site was sold to the federal government, who used it as a military training facility during World War II. In 1946, the ownership of the grounds reverted to the municipality. Beyond serving as a public gathering space and roller-skating rink, the 1951 installation of ice-making equipment transformed the building into the city's main arena, in which 3,500 fans can cheer for their local hockey teams.

The track for the city's Grand Prix motorsport race, launched in 1967, passes through the exhibition grounds, with the finish line located right in front of the Coliseum. Its present street address, on Gilles Villeneuve Avenue, pays homage to one of Canada's legendary racing car drivers.

ABOVE The exhibition ground's entrance gate, constructed in 1938, is an updated version of a Roman triumphal archway. Beyond its overall pyramidal massing and geometric arched openings, the gate's Zigzag detailing includes the prominent vertical stripes, the multiple-plane and step-back detailing on the piers, and the multitude of decorative panels. Directly above the central arch are bas-relief panels depicting a traditional Québécois homestead and a logging drive, while images of a spinning wheel and industrial machinery top the side entrances. Visible in the foreground are the sturdy barriers associated with the present-day motorsport track.